"Of all the small nations of this earth perhaps only the ancient Greeks surpass the Scots in their contributions to mankind."

Sir Winston Churchill

One thing Winston: whisky or ouzo?

- I rest my case

A LITTLE PREAMBLE

Oh, my goodness! How good is Scottish water straight from the tap?

Voted the most beautiful country in the world, Scotland topped the poll as the most stunning place on the planet. Who am I to disagree? We have mountains, lochs and castles to admire. Our cities are full of majestic buildings and baronial art. We have a grandiose infrastructure designed by Thomas Telford and the powerful architecture of Charles Rennie Mackintosh. We even have clean, pale-blue waters with white sandy beaches on which to sun ourselves - well, maybe not sun ourselves, but they are nice to peek at through the hood of an anorak.

In any one lifetime, it would be hard to visit every spot of interest in Scotland. There are over two thousand castles, hundreds of medieval churches, monasteries, museums and galleries. We have heritage centres, country parks, archaeological sites, distilleries, rivers, glens, nature reserves, and trails. Scotland has been around a long time - as you probably guessed, judging by the state of the roads.

Scotland is the home of golf, with more courses per head of population than anywhere else in the world, playing a different course every week would take over ten years to complete - or forever if you don't play golf.

Amid all the beauty are the big-hearted and entertaining Scots (translate that as 'patter merchants'). We have more than our fair share of talented people, inventors, comedians, poets, authors, sports stars, and actors. Is there anywhere else on earth with such a rich source of fascinating history, sights, and people?

I spent over thirty years policing a small part of Scotland and sometimes seeing the worst it offered. When I retired, I decided it was time for me to explore. It was nice to dispense with the uniform and talk to people who didn't look at me as if I had a massive plook growing out my forehead.

Along the way, I discovered many fascinating things.

I delved into our intriguing history and visited places that took my breath away. I found places that served thirst quenching beer and savoured whisky as good as a 15-year-old malt at half the price. I supped the tastiest soup, stayed in the cosiest B&B, and experienced food that delighted the taste buds. I enjoyed interesting walks, laughed at the banter, and I want to tell you all about it.

Not to be big-headed but you will probably enjoy this these tales because Scotland is full of treasures and it is worth coming just to taste the tap water.

Chapter one

IT'S NO NIAGARA FALLS, IS IT?

Hail to Callander, a flourishing triumph at the gateway to the Highlands.

North of Stirling, Callander bustles with tourists in the summer, a popular base for exploring Loch Lomond & The Trossachs National Park. The picturesque village the location for the original *Doctor Finlay's Casebook*. Despite the idyllic setting, my old colleague, Davy, challenged me to spot a smiling tourist. Once he drove me from one end of Callander to the other and I did not see so much as a grin. He is of the opinion all visitors to Callander have the same dour expression, as if they forgot to tell their faces they are supposed to be enjoying themselves.

Entering Callander on the A84, just before you reach the shops, there is a signpost giving directions to Bracklinn Falls. I drove my old second-hand Jag up the hill and onto the single track road. I powered the three-litre V6 past the Callander Crags walk, rising steeply for a quarter of a mile and into the Bracklinn Falls car park, fortunate not to meet any oncoming vehicles. This is where my luck ran out, the car park was full.

Callander is less famous for being the boyhood home of another of my old colleagues, PC Angus Penfold. I worked with Angus very early in my police service. Hilarious in his self-deprecation he always had a story to tell of some scrape he had gotten into. Angus is a magnet for mishaps.

1

There are people who are inattentive. If there is a puddle on the road, they inadvertently stand in it and get wet. There are others who are unlucky; they see the puddle, sidestep to avoid it and still get soaked as a car drives through the puddle and splashes them. PC Penfold is both inattentive and unlucky. He would jump the puddle to avoid getting wet, then land on a jobbie, slip and fall back into the puddle and then get splashed by the passing car. And that is kind of what happened when he talked to his Mum about her funeral arrangements.

His mother, aged ninety-two, was showing signs of infirmity and causing Angus some concern. Her fallibility induced him to broach the subject of her funeral, for no other reason than to establish if she had any preferences.

"Mum, I was thinking about the future."

"Yes, Angus."

"It's just that nobody lives forever and… well, I was just thinking… um."

"You were thinking we all won't live forever or just me?"

"Um, well… I'd just like to do you proud."

"Bit late for that Angus," she said with a cheeky smile.

"Oh Mum! I need to know what you would like at your funeral, you know hymns and things like that."

"You can play, 'Always Look on the Bright Side of Life' by Monty Python for all I'll care."

"Seriously Mum."

"Seriously, I won't be listening. It won't matter to me."

"Do you not have a favourite hymn?"

"I used to like Amazing Grace."

"Amazing Grace, okay."

"Until I fell out with my neighbour."

"You fell out with your neighbour?"

"Yes, Grace McNulty, she was a big fat pain in the backside. Ever since then I sang it as 'Always Grazing Grace',"

"Right so you don't mind what hymns you have?"

"No, son, I don't mind."

"Have you any thoughts about whether you want to be buried or cremated?"

"No, just surprise me."

"What about your eulogy, I think I will have to do that?"

"Well, you don't expect me to do it, do you?"

"Er, no Mum, but you could maybe give me a hand to write it."

"Sure, if I have the time."

"If you have the time?"

"Yes, I don't know if I will be able to fit it in."

"Fit it in before your funeral?"

"Yes, it depends on what date you have in mind?"

PC Penfold's mother may be infirm but there is nothing wrong with her mind.

In the time I took to relate the story to Mrs McEwan a Vauxhall exited the car park, I parked in the free space. Monkeydog jumped out from the back seat and sniffed out a place to pee.

Monkeydog is the mongrel we adopted. Abandoned as a pup, someone found him in a park and handed him into my police office. He was so cute. I had to pull rank to take him home. Now fully grown he is the size of a spaniel. He has the head of a terrier but we have never figured out what

3

breeds combined to make this smart and fiercely loyal dog. His coat grows wild like a Viking's beard and if left untended for too long he takes on the look of a miniature ginger sheep. A haircut transforms him back into a golden coloured pup again. We call him Monkeydog because he likes to climb onto walls and jump from gatepost to gatepost.

The Callander Crags walk is a circuit that takes you high above Callander through mixed woodland and up to the Jubilee Cairn. From the top there are sweeping views of the town and back to the untamed area of upland to the north. They erected the cairn to celebrate Queen Victoria's diamond jubilee. It sits on the Black Rock like an upturned cone dunked into the ground. It has an unusual white quartz rock sitting on the top like someone has put a dollop of ice-cream on the wrong end. It is a hearty walk but today we were doing the easier route to Bracklinn Falls.

There is a well-worn path to the falls. We set off, Mrs McEwan wrapped up in a scarf and gloves. I stuffed my hands into my pockets to fend off the chill. Monkeydog's tail wagged like he didn't care. We passed a group of young Americans. They might have been late teens or early twenties. About a dozen, all kitted out in proper walking gear. Heavy boots, big thick grey socks and the best of Gore-Tex jackets (XXL). We didn't pass them easily, not because they were keeping up a good pace - they weren't - but because they were walking two abreast and taking up the full width of the path. These were big kids. I did the old cough-cough trick to alert them to our presence and then wait on them waddling out of our way.

With no more sound barriers we heard the crash of water down below. Bracklinn Falls steps its way down

4

through the forest, the cold black water flecked with forest debris (Bracklinn is Gaelic for speckled pool). The waters were not in full flow but it is easy to imagine the Winter and Spring deluge tumbling, grinding and sculpting the rocks into a high-walled gorge. A flash flood in August 2004 swept away the previous iron bridge. In its place is a more substantial wooden construction arched well above the water. The wooden beams stretch up to form a covered roof in the middle and reminded me of a tepee. The bridge is in an ideal spot to take in the sight of the river tumbling over the steps upstream and shear sided walls as it quickly drops away downstream. A board has some interesting snippets of information including the fact this area is a frontier for red squirrels.

I used to think all squirrels were cute little nut grabbers. I've seen how smart they are. There was a TV programme that set up obstacle courses for them and they had to use their intelligence, dexterity and aptitude to figure out how to get to the nuts - which they invariably did. Squirrels are great animals to observe. If you watch them for long enough they suddenly seem to realise they are late for an appointment. They stop what they are doing, their head pops up in panic and they dash off to their meeting behind the back of a tree. Squirrels are shy creatures and will scurry off as soon as they see you - even quicker if you have a dog. Not that Monkeydog is a danger to them, he'd just want to climb trees with them and hang out.

The red squirrel is the UK's only native squirrel species. It was once widespread across the whole of Great Britain. Now they are in danger of being ousted by the Grey squirrel. Grey squirrels were introduced in the 1870s and, as they are larger than the red squirrel, have been on a march up the length of the UK out-competing our ginger breed for food and shelter. The Greys like to bully their smaller ginger cousins out of their homes and follow up with a nasty disease they carry, which kills the reds. Sadly, it is likely the red squirrel will become extinct within a generation.

With that in mind I kept my eyes open for a red squirrel. I was hoping to see one in the woods as we made our way to Bracklinn Falls. I didn't. Not a sniff of ginger. We decided the walk to the falls was all too brief, so we crossed the bridge and headed up the path to the Scout Pool. Standing on the middle of the bridge were two Scots laddies. I could tell they were Scottish just from looking at them. This was November and one of them was wearing shorts, T-shirt and a pair of well worn white gutties. The other had on a thin *Adidas* anorak, black trousers, white socks and black *Doc Martin* shoes. They shared a roll-up cigarette, as they stared down at the falls.

As I passed, I overheard a snippet of their conversation.

"Whit dae ye think, Tam?"

"Aboot whit?"

"Whit dae ye hink am talkin aboot ya dafty, the watter doon there."

"Well, it's no Niagara Falls is it?"

The things you overhear when you haven't got a bullwhip!

The path over the bridge allowed us to walk along the stony riverbed and then ascend up through the forest of pine where the tall trees blanked out the sun. Despite the steep slope either side of the path, the pines shot up true and straight. The forest floor a mass of dead pine needles. It was all at once beautiful and as eerie as a Stephen King novel.

Then I had a brainwave, a brilliant idea.

"Let's have some nooky!"

"What?"

"We could nip into the forest and have a little fun," I winked.

"NO!" Mrs McEwan's answer was out of her mouth before I could even finish. A little too emphatically for my likening. I felt chastised at the supersonic rebuff.

"Why not?" I asked after a few seconds introspection.

Mrs McEwan paused a moment as if to think up a reason before replying.

"What about Monkeydog?"

"We could tie him up behind a tree for three minutes," ever the optimist.

Monkeydog stopped sniffing the bracken and looked up at me as if to say, 'Really! You want to tie me up in this playground while you have a bonk?'

Doubly chastised I carried on through the dank forest in silence.

The trees came to a stop, and we were back in the sunlight. My mood lightened. I could see the path sweep back down to the river and at the bottom a bridge crossed the water at the Scout Pool. Before long we were there. The bridge is nothing more than a wooden platform. Wide enough to let a tractor cross but no more. There are no sides to stop anyone falling off. Monkeydog ran to the middle of the bridge, put his front paws on the edge and looked downstream. He looked as if he was contemplating a dive into the water. It was a survivable jump but once in the water there would be no way for him to get out. The current would carry him over the precipice into the Scout Pool. I didn't fancy going in after him. We both screamed for him to come away from the edge. We needn't have worried. Monkeydog isn't stupid. He turned back to us, tail wagging furiously, happy that his little prank had worked. I gathered he was just getting his own back for my suggestion we tie him up in the forest. Little monkey.

On the way back down we passed a Dad trying to coax his ten-year-old son out of the trees. The laddie had had enough walking for one day and wanted to sit on the pine floor and talk Christmas presents.

Further on we overtook an elderly couple, taking measured steps and holding hands. I wasn't sure if they were in love or just mindful of the slippery path. We agreed, between the four of us, that it was a lovely walk.

On the single track road back down to the car park the views opened out, and it was such a clear day we could see the seventeen miles all the way to the Wallace Monument. The loop back to our starting point is about three miles long and well worth the effort. Despite the frosty air, the exercise kept us warm and served to work up an appetite. We didn't see any little ginger balls of furry nut-loving fun, but the good thing was we saw no greys either.

I had researched dog friendly pubs in Callander and the one that came up tops on *TripAdvisor* was *The Lade Inn*. Carry on out through Callander and you will come to Kilmahog. The Lade Inn is on the left. We were lucky enough to grab a space in the busy car park. We weren't lucky enough to get a seat inside. It was busy, too popular a spot. I noted, on a leaflet inside the door, The Lade Inn had won the accolade of 'best informal eating place' from The Forth Valley Food

Link (whoever they are). I presume this is one of the reasons it was so busy. A couple with a beagle who entered just before us, couldn't get served either. On their recommendation we headed back into Callander to try the *Riverside Restaurant*, also dog friendly.

In the grounds of The Lade Inn, they have a *Real Ale Shop* and determined not to have a wasted journey I popped in to see what I could buy, but the door was locked. A sign said I should press a buzzer and someone from the pub would come. I didn't have the heart to press it because they were so busy inside.

The Meadows Car Park in Callander is a beautiful spot. It overlooks the River Teith, which meanders lazily on a flat flood plain. In spate, the River Teith often floods the car park all the way up to the Main Street. The river supports a large population of ducks, swans and pigeons. An ideal spot to eat tourist tidbits and procreate (the birds not the tourists).

The car park put me in a bad mood. It is a pay and display and charges £1.90 for two hours. I inserted two £1 coins in the slot and, as I suspected, no change was forthcoming. I fumed about being 'cheated' out of 10p, I mean who carries 90p in change? This may be the reason you never see a tourist smile in Callander.

The Riverside Inn rear entrance faces onto the car park near the exit, so you can't miss it. It advertised itself as dog friendly. And they weren't kidding. Every second table had a dog under it. Our attentive waiter couldn't have been nicer. He brought Monkeydog a chew and granted us a good efficient lunch service. The place is a little ragged around the edges but I didn't mind. They serve *Schiehallion* (Harveistoun Ale) so I didn't need the place fresh painted to enjoy it. We tried the burgers. Great big seeded rolls arrived with well cooked chunky chips and big onion rings. Not fine dining, you understand, but plentiful and more than edible. Just what we were looking for after our walk. It was so filling we did not need dinner that night - but I ate some, anyway.

Callander is very much a tourist village and in the height of summer it is hard to get a parking spot or even a seat in a café. A 19th century Gothic church stands in the town square although it no longer functions as a place of worship. Instead it is the headquarters for *The Clanranald Trust for Scotland*. The object of the trust is to preserve Scottish heritage and spread Scottish culture through entertainment and education. The Chief Executive of the organisation is Charlie Allan. Charlie is a tall, rugged looking man, with close cropped hair and a full beard that straggles down to his chest. At any of the events they organise you will see him dressed in his kilt, with a sheepskin wrapped around his shoulders and a scowl on his face. He would not look out of place on *Game of Thrones*. The trust brings Scottish History to life, through historical re-enactments and living history events.

There are the usual woollen shops and cafes on the Main Street in Callander, and the rather excellent *Mhor Bread & Tearoom* where I purchased a scrummy looking angel cake to take home to Number three son and a rather delicious Chilli and Cheese Sourdough bread for myself. The choice of sourdough bread is fantastic, potato and leek the speciality of the day. Super looking mini steak pies had me salivating, so I bought some of those too.

Callander is a pleasant enough place to while away an hour or two. The Romans thought so too and built a fort on the edge of town to ensure the natives stayed in the hills. The remains of their ancient hill fort is at Dunmore overlooking Loch Venachar. I suspect that, come winter, the Scottish winds passing through their sandals was enough for the Romans to up sticks and leave.

For the more energetic visitor there are cycle routes and walks to challenge everyone. The best pint of beer I ever had was after an eighty mile cycle from Drumochter Pass down to Callander. A tasty pint of *Schiehallion* that hardly touched the sides.

I organised a much harder cycle with a group of friends from work. The route would take us from Callander through the Trossachs and past all the quiet lochs and mysterious woods. Cycling the vast countryside until we ended up back in Stirling. A journey of one hundred miles. Before we even got to the bottom of the first hill Donald came off his bike. We had worked up a sweat getting to the top, then experienced the death defying speed of the downhill. Donald hit a pothole, he lost control and hurtled from his bike smashing his elbow on the hard tarmac shattering it into fifty different pieces. The left side of his face scraped along the ground ripping half his skin away. Two following cars, bombing along behind us, narrowly missed running over him. It was bad enough. I got him to the side of the road and he lay there with blood in his eyes unable to see the extent of the damage to his elbow.

"Is it bad?" he asked, knowing full well it was.

I looked at his elbow. It was hanging limp at his side and a gaping hole had appeared. I could see into all the crushed bone and gristle. It was bad, it was worse than bad. I wondered if he would ever make full use of his arm again.

"It's just a scratch," I reassured him, "you'll be fine."

11

"Are you sure? It doesn't feel fine."

"Well, in fairness, it might put paid to your cricket career."

"Oh! That's okay then. I don't like cricket, anyway."

True to form, in times of trauma, police officers use humour to lighten the mood. It is a necessary part of good mental health. I know officers who have suffered from Post Traumatic Stress Disorder. Some had to leave the job, some suffered in silence. Police officers deal with many horrible things that can cause anxiety. Humour is a vital intervention. It helps ease the disquiet that can creep into our heads. Donald and I played the game. His elbow got fixed, they put a piece of metal in there to do the job for him and took skin grafts from his legs to cover it up. It still looks a mess on the outside but there isn't a mess inside his head because he laughed it off. Humour can take some of the pain away in the short term but it can also take all the pain away in the long term.

I went with Donald to hospital. The rest of the guys cycled to the nearest pub. We never did that cycle again.

Callander Police Office sits at the end of a side street down by the river. It is a small base from where the local officers patrol a large area. The beat extends into the Trossachs and covers all the lochs and mountains. The station attracts officers who have a passion for the outdoors. The officers who work there become a part of the community, they involve themselves in events and build strong relationships with the locals.

PC Gordon Mackay always wanted to work in Callander. He hiked, climbed, camped, and canoed in his spare time. His initial station, a busy, traffic clogged city, was not to his liking. As soon as Gordon completed his probation, he submitted a request for a move to Callander. The bosses approved his transfer. Two weeks later Gordon arrived nice and early for his first day at his new station. He changed into his uniform and introduced himself to everyone at the office. He spent the morning familiarising himself with local crimes, catching up on paperwork and chatting to his new colleagues.

In the afternoon his sergeant suggested they go for a drive. PC MacKay put on his hat and took a seat in the Landrover. His sergeant drove him to Inversnaid, the furthest point from the office still on their beat. A two hour round trip. All the time he talked to Gordon about the area, the problems, his experiences and the expectations he had of his cops. A leadership technique and a lesson in good management. They returned to the office at 3 p.m., just in time for Gordon to finish duty.

Gordon changed back into his civilian clothes; T-shirt, jeans, and trainers. As it was a sunny afternoon, rather than head straight home, he went for a walk in the town.

Gordon sauntered along the main street. He noticed how friendly people were, they smiled at him and said, "Hello," or "Good afternoon." Not what he was used to at his old station where people either ignored him or scowled.

Gordon passed the local bookmaker and popped in to make a bet on the weekend football games. When he handed his betting slip over, the lady behind the counter smiled at him and said, "You must be our new police officer?"

"Yes," he said, impressed that she knew who he was.

Gordon continued his walk. He stopped in at the butchers shop and bought sausage. The butcher, smiled heartily and said, "You must be the new bobby?"

"Yes, I am Gordon, PC Gordon MacKay. I just started today."

"Welcome to the town," said the butcher.

It impressed Gordon that the butcher knew who he was. Callander must have the best grapevine in the world. He had only driven to the end of his beat with his sergeant and already people knew who he was. This is a tight knit community, he thought.

Gordon stopped at the bakers and purchased rolls for his sausage. The shop assistant popped them in a bag and as she handed them over said, "So, you will be the new policeman in the town then?"

" Yes, I am Gordon, PC Gordon MacKay." somewhat confused. "Do you mind me asking how you knew?"

"You still have your police hat on," she smiled.

Chapter two

UP THE TROSSACHS

The problem with Scotish people is we, as a nation, are too generous. We provide our visitors with porridge, oatcakes, shortbread, haggis, neeps and tatties in abundance. However, often these go unappreciated. Visitors, I find, are much happier eating burgers and chips. Although, they all love traipsing through the charming views we can offer, such as beyond Callander and into the Trossachs National Park. The Trossachs is an area of outstanding beauty, a place for walkers, cyclists, canoeists, adventurers, fishermen and the occasional fruitcake (aka rock climbers). If it wasn't for the midges, thistles, jaggy nettles, and the effort it takes - tourists would overrun the place.

We have thousands of lochs; they are our gift to the world. Scotland's answer to the Lake District. We have Lochs: Katrine, Achray, Venachar, Lubnaig, Earn, Voil, Doine - you can look up the rest, but my favourite one is Loch Drunkie, just for its name. We have large fjord-like sea lochs, great fresh-water lochs, out of the way moorland puddles but only one 'lake'.

The little Lake of Menteith in the Trossachs received its status by mistake. In the 16th century a Dutch mapmaker was documenting Scotland and asked locals the name of the water. The locals thought he wanted to know what the area was called and told him he was in the laich of Menteith, 'laich' meaning low land. The Dutch map maker misunderstood and thought they were talking about the loch.

He recorded the body of water as the Lake of Menteith and it stuck.

It is not a deep loch, so it freezes over during arctic winters. It happened in 2010 (for the first time in thirty years), but they cancelled the planned 'bonspiel' or curling tournament due to fears for public safety. We were not so health and safety conscious a few decades ago. Curlers came from far and wide to head out onto the frozen water and spin their stones up and down the ice. Climate change has seen to the repeated failure of the ice to thicken enough to support such activity, that's if it freezes over at all.

The Lake of Menteith has a small island called Inchmahome, the site of the Inchmahome Priory. An idyllic sanctuary for quiet prayer and reflection. Inchmahome means Isle of Malcolm or *Malky's Island*, as I prefer. I think I might have liked to have spent a week or two in such a haven of peace and tranquillity. Growing my food and fishing for my dinner. Although, you could probably keep all the prayer and chanting that went on.

It is possible to visit Inchmahome. Historic Scotland ferry people across on a small motor boat from the boat-shed at Port of Menteith, they include in the price of admission. On the pier there is a wooden board that visitors have to turn so the white side faces the island. The ferryman will then know he has people to transport across the water. At the priory, now a ruin, it is easy to imagine how impressive it once was. Great thick walls and arched entries are impressive. I have often wondered how the builders could manage such a feat of construction all those centuries ago and also why they abandoned such a once magnificent place and left it to fall into ruin. My knowledgable friend, Davy, tells me this was down to the Protestant Reformation which led to a change in the laws and staus - thus the church could no longer extort land rents from poor frightened souls over whom they had so much influence.

The island has abundant wildlife and sweet-smelling flowers, with one exception. There is a boxwood bower, a set of trees, planted by Mary Queen of Scots when she was a mere bairn. I didn't know what a boxwood bower was, so I went in search. They might look nice elsewhere but the one on Inchmahome is a straggly looking thing and smelled of dust. I could take it or leave it. Mary might have been better planting something more useful - like Marijuana, you know something that might take the edge off all the praying and chanting.

I had a pleasant trip to Inchmahome. In Port of Menteith, there is the *Nick Nairn Cookery School* where you can take a class and learn to cook the perfect steak with white chocolate brulee or you could just go to the *Port of Menteith Hotel* where you can get a super Sunday lunch. The Port of Menteith Hotel looks like a nice place for an overnight stop, a place where you could sit outside and admire the lake with a glass of wine (midges permitting). I didn't go in. I had other sights to see. I headed on to Rob Roy MacGregor country of Loch Achray and Loch Katrine.

Robert Roy MacGregor, known as Rob Roy or Red MacGregor was a famous folk hero. A Scottish Robin Hood, according to Daniel Defoe who immortalised him in his book, making him a legend in his own lifetime. Sir Walter Scott fleshed out Rob Roy's biography a century later adding to his fame.

In the 1953 film, *Rob Roy the Highland Rogue,* our hero was played by Richard Todd and in the 1995 film, named simply *Rob Roy,* Liam Neeson played the lead. Neither Todd nor Neeson are Scottish, both being born in Northern Ireland. (At least they weren't from Oz - you know who I mean).

Rob Roy was a ginger; hence Red McGregor. He was born near Loch Katrine, third son of a clan chief. He was by turn a soldier, businessman, cattle-rustler and outlaw. His foray into soldiering came during the Jacobite uprising. Jacobites were small cracker baked foods that were particularly tasty when topped with cheese and relish. Wait, I'm thinking of Jacobs Cream Crackers.

My shorthand version: The Jacobite Rebellion all started when Charles Edward Stuart, aka 'Bonnie Prince Charlie', planned a hostile takeover of the country. Bonnie Prince Charlie believed the British throne to be his birthright and persuaded his Jacobite followers to help him remove the Hanoverian 'usurper' George II. Loyalty and religion played its part. Although, it wasn't all Catholics against the Protestants. George had followers from both persuasions, who were happy that under him the country was a good going concern. Money rules.

Both Rob Roy and his father fought at the Battle of Killiecrankie. Rob Roy was only eighteen, despite the death of their leader they won the battle. That wasn't the end of it. Within a year, Dunkeld and Cromdale had staged further battles. There have been many battles before and since, right through to the Battle of the Braes in 1882. The Highland Clearances were almost over when crofters on Skye decided to fight the government. The crofters refused to pay their rents and had a violent barny with the police who tried to serve them with eviction notices, sparking the last battle fought on Britsh soil. *For all that the Scots are a cheery and*

18

hospitable bunch, ye'll aye find somebody with a lang memory who still holds a grudge.

Rob returned to the Trossachs and farmed cattle. He prospered and gained a reputation as a trustworthy businessman. To make his fortune, he borrowed £1,000 from the Duke of Montrose, a landowner based at Mugdock Castle near Milngavie*, to purchase cattle intending to rear them for the following year's market. That must have been a vast sum of money. I did a rough calculation based on the yearly average wage at the time and I reckon in today's money the loan would have been worth around £2.5 million. Such a sum was too much of a temptation for the head drover who somehow stole it from Rob Roy. Fortunately for the drover, Rob Roy wasn't able to find him or I imagine his head wouldn't have stayed attached to his body for long, Rob Roy being well-known for his long arms and being handy with a sword.

Why is Milngavie pronounced MullGuy?
I looked it up. The mismatch between the town's written and pronounced name stems from the way its Gaelic name, **Muileann Dhaibahidh** *(I kid you not) was adapted into English. I read the explanation three times and to be honest, I'm none the wiser. Don't even get me started on Kirkcudbright (Kir Coo Bree) or Menzies (Ming'us). The most difficult to pronounce place in Scotland, I think, is the little hamlet of* **Achluachrach** *near Roybridge in Inverness-shire, which sounds the same as when you have a heavy cold and you clear your throat of a particularly troublesome blob of phlegm.*

The Duke of Montrose wasn't best pleased either. He blamed Rob Roy, bankrupted him, evicted his family from their home and seized his lands. Rob Roy turned to banditry. He stole cattle from the Duke of Montrose and robbed his factors. Our ginger Robin Hood took to his new career with aplomb. He started a mafia-like business of offering 'protection' to other landowners and stealing from those who didn't pay up.

Nothing romantic about a protection racket, is there?

Most of the stories of Rob's derring-do come from this period. Rob was also active in the Jacobite rebellions around this time. In the confrontation between the government and the Jacobites, the main fighting took place at the *Battle of Sheriffmuir* in 1715, when some historians believe Rob Roy went off on a special mission for the Earl of Mar, who was in charge of the Jacobite forces. Rob returned too late to the field to affect the outcome of this indecisive battle. His activity (or lack of it) on the day has been a cause for historical controversy – with Sir Walter Scott suggesting, in a suspect introduction to his novel, that *Rob Roy* was only interested in plundering and thus kept clear of the action.

Aye, Ginger MacGregor may have been a lot of things, but he wasn't stupid!

As a police inspector, Central Scotland Police stationed me at Stirling for a while and made me responsible for critical incidents covering all of Stirlingshire. Stirling City and the nearby towns and villages took up most of my focus. It was rare for me to make the trip out west to the Trossachs, the further reaches of my beat. It took too much time. The journey to Inversnaid in the Trossachs, for example, is a winding road, up one side of a loch and down the other. A pleasant enough drive but it could take up most of an eight-hour shift. Thus, when serious incidents happened out west, I relied on the local sergeants and cops.

On one occasion a call came in from a holidaymaker who had seen what appeared to be an unexploded shell lying in two feet of water at the side of a loch. The only road in and out of the area ran next to the side of the loch twenty yards away from where the shell protruded from the water. The officer in attendance passed a description of the shell and asked, "What do you want done, inspector?"

I had to go on the facts presented. The holidaymaker had showed a young cop to the location, the closest he could get to the device, without getting wet, was about ten feet. The young cop confirmed the device he saw poking out of the water looked very much like the tip of an explosive shell. It was cylindrical with a pointy end, about three inches wide. He estimated it to be about twelve to eighteen inches long. What to do?

Here is more information for you:-

It was evening and would be dark in about two hours.

The road served three towns and some small villages.

About two hundred cars, vans and lorries would pass by the side of the loch every hour. It might be quieter during the night, but it would get busy again by first light.

The EOD (Explosive Ordinance Disposal Unit) would not arrive until the next day.

The shortest detour for cars unable to use the road was a distance of one hundred and forty miles.

So you see the problem.

The sergeant in charge of the area was only about half an hour away when the call came in, he arrived just as the cop radioed in what he observed. The sergeant had already decided on an exclusion zone and instructed that no-one was to approach the device, cops were to stay off the shore and remain on the roadway at least twenty yards away and ensure cars could pass. Here is a tip for all supervisors in these situations. Cops need to do something even if it is nothing.

"Stay there and make sure nobody gets closer than twenty yards."

Now they are doing something.

A second tip in these situations is - extend the cordon or exclusion zone. Let's face it; I don't know if twenty yards is a safe enough distance for cops to stand or for cars to pass. I wasn't about to find out. I radioed in my instructions.

"I want an exclusion zone of one hundred yards either side of the device."

"Inspector, that means we will have to block the road and turn traffic back."

"That's correct. Do it, and do it now. Nobody is to go anywhere near the device, and I mean nobody. Nobody is to drive past on that road, not without my express permission."

Now they had something to do. They had to figure out how to go about it, and that would keep them busy. Be clear about what they have to do. They will do nothing much, but they will do nothing much with a purpose.

Minutes later the sergeant sent me a picture of the device via his mobile phone. It looked like an explosive shell, I had no reason to doubt it could be dangerous. I was right to believe the description given by the cop and my decision to extend the exclusion zone was spot on. No-one would die on my watch.

Two minutes later the sergeant called me on my radio.

"It's okay Inspector; it's just a toy."

"A what?"

"It is the head of a plastic toy. It just looked like a shell when it was sitting in the water."

The sergeant had put on a pair of wellies and waded out to see what it was. He used a pencil to tip it up and only then did he realise it was just a toy. On the one hand, I was glad he had resolved the situation, on the other it miffed me he had ignored my instructions.

"Bring it to my office and let me see it please."

I didn't need to see it, but I decided his two-hour round trip would be his punishment for ignoring my instructions not to go anywhere near the device. I didn't need to give him a telling off. When he arrived, I gave him a great big pat on the back for his initiative.

It is one thing that happens from time to time. Situations arise that create problems which can escalate into major incidents. Along comes a practical sergeant and solves it before we spend a lot of time and money causing public inconvenience, disrupting transport and missed ferries. They might go against orders or procedures but, ultimately, they have the best interests of the job at heart. On those occasions, I found it best not to make a fuss.

The Trossachs is a place where everything in the world is where it should be. Here you can be Sir Edmund Hillary, without having to have a Sherpa guide. Ben A'an, for example, at 1,500 feet, is an hour's brisk walk to the top. The route from the south side starts at the car park off the A821by the shores of Loch Achray. It soon winds up amongst the steep crags above the cut back woods. Volunteers have crafted an excellent giant's staircase from rocks, making it an achievable climb for anyone with a modicum of fitness. The route disappears into a narrow gully until you get almost under the summit, gained by a last rocky section. There it rewards you with views to take your breath away - so catch a mouthful of air before you make that last short climb.

The view includes Loch Katrine, the Trossachs, and surrounding mountains. A sight that well repays the effort in getting there. Below you can see the Sir Walter Scott. At nearly 120 years old, the Steamship Sir Walter Scott still plies the waters of Loch Katrine to this day. It's route marked by its wash ploughing a furrow to both shores.

The Sir Walter Scott is the only steamship on a fresh water loch in Scotland. At the time it was quite a feat of engineering to get the boat to Loch Katrine. Assembled with nuts and bolts at Denny's shipyard in Dumbarton, the pieces were numbered and dismantled before being transported by barge up Loch Lomond and overland by horse and cart to Stronachlachar Pier and there rebuilt and launched. It now sails the loch that supplies Glasgow's drinking water.

In the mid 1800s Glasgow desperately needed a good, clean water supply. Diseases were rife, including typhoid, cholera, dysentery, and alcohol poisoning (the latter more to do with over indulgence in our national drink). They needed tens of millions of gallons of water every day. The city's fathers identified Loch Katrine as capable of supplying that need, but the problem they had was how to get the water from there to Glasgow. The answer was something that is in infinite supply and doesn't cost a penny; gravity.

Glasgow Corporation put three thousand men to work building a pipe connected by aqueducts and tunnels to the city over thirty miles away. This was an impressive feat of engineering. In order for it to work they had to make sure the pipe dropped ten inches for every mile of its length. If there was a hill in the way they went straight through it and out the other side. Then they had to build a dam to raise the water levels and ensure a continuous supply. They finished all the work in an impressive three years.

In charge of the project was a young engineer called John Bateman, at the completion of the project he said, "I leave you a work, which I believe will, with very slight attention, remain perfect for ages, which for the greater part of it, is as indestructible as the hills." And Bateman was right, this wonderful piece of engineering has remained perfect for ages.

And who knew Glaswegians drank water?

My latest trip to the summit of Ben A'an found the path well walked with tourists sharing a cheery word or two as they passed in the opposite direction. Those going down extolled the virtues of reaching the top with a gloaty wee smile. Smug knowing that those going up had the hard part to do.

At the top of Ben A'an we rested and waited patiently for a young couple to take a thousand selfies before they got out of the way and we could take our pictures. My boys used their phones to photograph each other attempting handstands on the summit, imagining their pictures would be original - I think they were. The results were impressive.

Monkeydog scampered around with energy, disinterested in joining the family photo. Mrs McEwan dished out a boiled sweet, I negotiated the wrapper and placed the mint humbug in my mouth. There is something agreeable about sucking on a sugary treat at the top of a mountain. A small reward for a big effort but immensely satisfying.

Our hike to the top bred confidence. The descent made us feel like mountain goats. We hopped and skipped down the path, spurred on by the fresh air, the view and the thought of replacing lost fluids with a pint.

The road back to Callander skirts Loch Achray, which is one of the most charming little lochs in Scotland, when seen from its eastern end. At its head commences an unsurpassed mix of purple crag, silver-grey birch, oak copse, and green pasture. Ben Venue rises behind it, broken, rugged, steep and dangerous, it adds a majesty to the scene exceeding what its actual height would lead you to think. It is, perhaps, the glossiest mountain in Scotland, surpassing anything you might see in the Lake District of England. Ben Venue is as different from the ordinary run of Scottish mountains as the pelt of an otter to the hide of a rhino.

We stopped at the small hamlet of Brig O'Turk and popped into the *Brig O'Turk Tea Room.* A small place, just a wooden hut, painted green with a felt roof. Oh Boy! What a delight, the smell of roasted coffee and fresh baked cakes had us salivating as soon as we entered. It was busy and we had to take our refreshments outside to a wooden table and bench, which was fine because Monkeydog saw a sign barring him from entry. I've been to the Brig O'Turk Tea Room a few times and enjoyed waddling away with a belly full of cake on each occasion.

One time I was there to pick up number three son who had been walking the hills for three days with a group who were prepping for their Duke of Edinburgh Award. It wasn't a pleasant day; the rain had started in earnest. I rushed into the Tea Room, placed my order for coffee and cake and explained that my dog was in the car so I'd better take it out there, "I'll bring it out to you she said." And she did. The waitress delivered my coffee and cake to my car, smiling, despite the teeming rain.

Since then, if passing, I always stopped at the *Brig O'Turk Tea Room*. Hence my disappointment this year to find it closed. Why is it when I find a decent place to eat, it burns down, changes hands or the Environmental Health condemn the place?

I did a little detective work. It was none of those three.

The rumour is the people behind the Tea Room were doing well, they spruced up the place and took pride in the food and service. They approached their landlord and asked if he would sell them the building. He refused.

'Watch out! Be on your guard against all kinds of greed; a man's life does not consist in the abundance of his possessions.'

Instead of heeding the words of the Bible, the landlord saw an opportunity to put the rent up. Instead of selling them the hut he took advantage of their hard work and squeezed them for more money. He took Gordon Gekko's saying to heart, 'Greed, for lack of a better word, is good.'

Except it isn't.

Greed is a bottomless pit. The more you strike deeper the harder it is to get out. Greed exhausts all attempts of a saviour. It leaves you with nothing but a hole. Or, in the case of this landlord, a small wooden hut, with peeling green paint and a deteriorating felt roof. That is all that is there now. The increase in rent became the last straw and the people left.

I imagine the landlord stopping by his premises every day and lamenting his decision. Instead of providing a steady income, his disused hut is empty and rotting.

The Trossachs is a vastly interesting place. It is possible to spend days wandering the hills or camping at the side of a loch. Thus it attracts a lot of visitors from all over the world. I welcome them. Such beauty is only worth anything when shared. Alas, this is where some men earn their 'vile' description, for the manner in which they dispose of cigarette packets, beer cans and plastic wrappings.

In warm weather, those in the cities and towns cross their doorsteps and take to the Trossachs. They are not content to wander through the wilds without setting a fire and downing copious amounts of cheap wine and beer. Leaving their mess at their backsides. They have even been known to leave behind their tents, sleeping bags and camping equipment.

They have no pride in their country, it is nothing short of a disgrace.

The police have organised patrols to combat these despicable people for years. One innovative sergeant took it upon himself to rid the Trossachs of these shameless rogues. In normal circumstances officers would find an encampment and warn those present to clear up their rubbish. The next day the rogues would be gone but their rubbish remained. Instead, the sergeant, took a picture of the area and the rogues. He then took their details and charged them with littering.

"I will return tomorrow. If you leave a single fag end behind, I will submit a report to the Procurator Fiscal and they will fine you. Save yourself some money and clear up your mess."

Unfortunately, the area is too large to patrol in its entirety, only a small percentage are dealt with in this way and the problem remains. It is perhaps the midge who does a better job than the police.

The Scottish midge is a pesky little chap, especially on the west coast where the wet soil, bogs and mires are ideal breeding grounds. Pound for pound, a midge packs a bigger punch than Mike Tyson. It has a wingspan of 1.4 mm and a weight of 0.5 micrograms, yet for their small size they are the irredeemable hooligans of the Highlands. Scientists discovered that they use their heads to gyrate like a jigsaw power tool and force its sharp jaws deep into the skin. They are the ultimate blood-sucking machines and can go on to gorge double their body weight in blood before flying off. A swarm of them can inflict three-thousand bites in an hour.

If it wasn't for the midges maybe we'd have more campers and the mess would be worse.

Chapter three

WI A BIT O' LUCK

St. Fillans, named after an Irish missionary, is a delightful little village of cottages and homes which lies along the eastern end of Loch Earn within Loch Lomond and the Trossachs National Park. There are only about two hundred houses clustered in a narrow strip around the north side of the loch and the outlet of the the river. Despite it having so few occupants, it has its own nine-hole golf course, and that was where I was headed.

If you are travelling from Stirling, I would recommend turning onto the B827, just after Braco. That slightly cuts the distance down but not the time. It is an enjoyable road winding through the hills, past places like Tigh Na Blair and Cultybraggan Camp.

Cultybraggan Camp has an interesting history. It was used during WW2 as a maximum-security Prisoner of War camp and incarcerated some of the most dangerous Nazis ever captured. Cultybraggan was known as a 'black-camp' housing the SS diehards who swore death before surrender. They sent here a group of ringleaders, described as 'the most callous of men,' who had been responsible for an attempted mass breakout at a camp in England. Believing someone had betrayed them, they turned on one of their own and beat him to death. They hadn't been betrayed, they had been caught out by the oldest trick in the book. One of the guards spoke German and overheard their plot to escape. The five prisoners responsible were hanged for their crime, in what was the largest multiple execution in 20th-century Britain. After the war Cultybraggan became an army

30

training camp and although some 100 Nissan huts were demolished to make way for a firing range many remain. The Comrie Development Trust purchased the land in 2007 and the camp is now open to visitors and is used by the local community for business.

Even amongst the most callous of men are people who can lift the spirits. Collectively, we can be driven to the most horrible acts. Individually, we are a mix of both good and bad. Heinrich Steinmeyer was held as a prisoner of war at Cultybraggan Camp. A member of Hitler's notoriously fanatical SS Waffen division. Captured in France by a Scottish regiment a year before the end of the war. On being told to empty his pockets he placed two apples on the ground. The Scottish soldier had a look at the apples and gave them back to him with the words, "You will need them."

Before leaving France his group of prisoners were attacked by French civilians wielding butcher knives. The Scottish soldiers drove them off. On the ferry to Southampton the Scottish soldiers saved him again, this time from a group of Poles with pocket knives. This happened frequently on the journey to Cultybraggan Camp.

"I was lucky to be captured by the Scots," he said, moved by the unexpected way his captors treated him. After the war, Heinrich remained in Scotland for seven years, staying in hostels and working as a farmhand. He may well have stayed in Scotland if he had not had to go back to Germany to look after his elderly mother.

Heinrich Steinmeyer died in 2014, he left his entire estate, a not inconsiderable £384,000, for the benefit of the older people of Comrie. The Comrie Development Fund have taken charge of his legacy. An act of gratitude for the kindness the Scottish people showed during his time in Scotland.

Seldom in life do we regret an act of compassion.

I passed through Comrie before entering the village of St Fillans, the Golf Club entrance hides to the left. So how does a golf course within such a small village survive? I arrived at 9 a.m. on a Monday morning in September. The rain had clattered down all day on Sunday and through most of the night, but the forecast said I would more-or-less find it dry. The club was surprisingly busy. Groups of four seniors spattered the fairways and tees. The membership clearly liked to get out early in the morning - and get back in again before the rain started.

I was playing in a retired police competition, the Jimmy McFadyen Trophy. I didn't know Jimmy McFadyen; he must have been a decent fellow because his colleagues donated a trophy in his memory. I noticed the trophy was, in fact, a silver plate and that Jimmy McFadyen was the first to win it.

'1998 Jimmy McFadyen'

I'm still not sure how that worked; maybe they awarded it to him posthumously, remembering a cracking round of golf he played in the past. I didn't find out because Jimmy McFadyen wasn't the main topic of conversation, the guys who knew him preferred to talk about his wife - and not in a good way. Mrs McFadyen, it would appear, was quite the battleaxe. Brian, one of my playing partners, regaled us with a story about how his six-year-old daughter had run home 'greetin' because Mrs McFadyen had taken an altogether stern approach with her for being one decibel too loud. Brian wasn't best pleased with the unwarranted scolding his daughter had received.

Harry told us how he had forgotten to invite Mrs McFadyen to present the prize one year. She had erupted like Mount Vesuvius and taken such a huff they decided to send ex-Inspector McTool to her house to placate her. Ex-Inspector McTool wasn't renowned for his soft skills; he has varyingly been described as an ignorant, bullying, blustering buffoon. Sometimes all in the one sentence and once 'to the highest order'. Mrs McFadyen never came back, she deferred the job of presenting the trophy to one of her sons. He is a nice fella, so it worked out for the best.

Despite St Fillans Golf Course being in the middle of the Central Highlands, it is quite flat. The course nestles into the flat plain of a valley between two imposing ranges of hills that are both dark and handsome. I was in awe. The course isn't long but has some tricky dog-legs. I was struck by the serenity of the place. It is hard to pull your eyes away from the magnificent scenery, therefore easy to miss your opponent's ball drop into the rough. Any help provided in finding it is like the blind leading the blind.

I was thoroughly enjoying the course, not just because I hadn't played it before, but mainly as I was playing well. That was until the seventh hole. A long par five which had a drystane dyke marking the out-of-bounds all the way up the left side of the fairway. It was so intimidating I sliced my ball into the trees on the right. Over the drystane dyke is a waterhole and reed bed that is home to some large bird, probably a goose. It constantly honked a strange double-barrelled guffaw. I swear it was laughing at my shot, then again at my next and the one after that. It guffawed at me as

I duffed every shot all the way up to the green where I gave in and picked up my ball.

St Fillans is only a nine hole course, so to complete the round we had to play each hole twice. During the second nine, the rain came across the valley in a sheet and caused a flurry of activity as we fetched our waterproof jackets from our bags and tried to get our umbrellas up all at the same time. The rain didn't last long but was replaced by a fearsome crosswind. No longer did I think of the course as tranquil. The blustery wind destroyed the fun I was having conquering this new course. My two efforts at the same nine holes could not have been more different. Maybe the locals knew what to expect because at the half-way point there was no sign of any groups of seniors anywhere. Whether or not their golf was complete, they had simply buggered off before the squall.

I was glad to get the seventeenth and have the clubhouse and a hot coffee in sight. A greenkeeper was working on the tee, he stopped what he was doing, lit a roll-up cigarette and exchanged pleasantries with us in such a languid fashion it made me think there was more than just tobacco in his roll-up.

A greenkeeper who likes grass, what are the chances?

We made it back to the clubhouse, a basic elongated wooden shed. I dumped my clubs in the boot of my car and eagerly made my way in for some food. The coffee and bacon roll we had before the game was adequate as was the fish and chips and sticky toffee pudding served by the club for our afternoon lunch. There were only twelve of us, and we all had soft drinks but it all adds to the clubs coffers. Maybe they will survive another year. I hope so. If you enjoy golf, St Fillans is worth playing. It isn't too taxing, and good players can score well.

Afterwards, I jumped into my car and turned left out of the driveway to explore the village. As I entered, the waters of Loch Earn opened out to my left. The scenery is remarkably fine. Several small boats were tethered to buoys about fifty yards out and bobbed about on the windblown loch; I wondered how the owners got out to them. The wind made the loch look tidal. It made for a nice view, but I'd pass at taking a hurl in one of those boats in anything less than calm sunny weather.

Arrans Loch Earn Brewery, Coffee Shop, Hotel & Visitor Centre was blazoned on a sign over the first large stone building on the right. Opposite, by the side of the loch, some heavy wooden tables and chairs sat on a patch of grass and declared itself to be the 'Beer Garden'. I stopped my car in the car park next to it. The car park is shaded by twin oak trees called the Goose Oaks, planted in 1818 over the interred remains of a goose that is said to have lived for 106 years. Not only did this goose have magical powers of longevity but it warned the Clan Neish, then occupying the site of St Fillans, of the approach of the hostile McNabs. Maybe it is still alive and resettled next to the 7th hole at the golf course - its guffaw warning me the yips are coming.

Unsurprisingly, the car park and beer garden were empty. It was a Monday in September, remember. There was now a cold wind that put me off venturing out of the car. The hotel looked inviting, but I didn't need coffee or a snack, so I continued further through the village. I was scuppered in my tracks by those logs they put down to identify individual parking spaces. The ones you can't see from your car. *Why do they do that?* Just tarmac the thing and paint lines or put nothing down that will chip the paintwork of your customer's cars. They are a hazard. Fortunately, it was my front tyre that connected with the log, and all that happened was my car pushed the log out of position. Anyone coming in from the other side would now undoubtedly have the same problem.

Further through the village, they have lots of lay-bys at the side of the loch. It is easy to pull in and admire the view and the ducks as they wait patiently at the side of the road for the occasional tourist scrap. I imagine their pickings from picnics in the summer are plentiful, but I bet they have it rough in winter.

Almost at the end of the village is a large hotel called *The Four Seasons*. There wasn't much activity, but it looked like it does a decent plate of fish and chips.

I later read that in 2005 the village had been the centre of some controversy when the local council halted the building of a housing development to avoid killing the fairies (*yes I checked the date, it was definitely in 2005*). The locals complained that if the developer moved a big rock, it would 'upset' the fairies who lived underneath it. There was such an uproar they summoned the developer to a community council meeting where chairman Jeannie Fox told him she believed in fairies although she couldn't be sure they lived under that rock.

If the locals want to believe in fairies, then it is up to them, I suppose.

What transpired was an agreement that the standing stones and large rocks couldn't be moved to accommodate the build. At an extra cost of thousands of pounds the new development centres on a small park with the 'fairy' rock in the middle. I'm not sure where the fairy rock is in St Fillans, maybe I missed the signs. Such things make a place so much more interesting and I'm all for play parks and large rocks. Had I known about it before, I would have looked to pay it a visit. Maybe the fairies would have popped out to prove me a cynic.

Finally, I about turned and once again stopped outside the Arrans Loch Earn Brewery, Coffee Shop, Hotel & Visitor Centre with the purpose of adjusting my sat nav so I could make my way home via Comrie, Crieff and Auchterarder. One of the staff members inside, a lady in her late fifties with a stressed looking face, toddled on out to see if I was lost and in need of directions. I thought it very nice of her.

"What kind of beer do you brew?" I asked after explaining I didn't require directions.

"Well, wur no actually brewin' anyhing the noo. It's still getting built oot the back," she informed me.

That news was a bit of a surprise because the sign proudly displayed the fact that there was a brewery there and I hadn't disbelieved it.

"When will it be ready?"

"Och, sometime next year. Wi' a bit o' luck."

"With a bit of luck?"

"Aye, we'll need a bit of luck, but he says he will get it up an runnin."

I presumed the 'he' she was referring to was the owner, and surmised there might be money issues.

"So you are just a coffee shop and a hotel, just now?"

"Naw, we had a fire. We canny have any guests the noo. We need a bit o' luck to get it back open again, ye ken."

"You had a fire?"

"Aye, the hotel got aw burnt."

"But you still have the coffee shop and a bar I take it?"

"Oh aye, we have the coffee shop, but we can only open the bar on a Thursday, Friday and Saturday."

"You can only open the bar on a Thursday, Friday and Saturday, why?"

"Because I'm the only wan wi a personal licence and I only work those days."

I was about to point out she was working right now and today was a Monday when a young couple wearing hiking boots passed behind the only personal licence holder of the Arrans Loch Earn Brewery and made their way into the coffee shop.

"Och, customers," she said, about turned and followed them in.

It looked like they would be the only two customers that day.

"I wish you luck then," I shouted after her. I think the place was probably going to need it. Winter would mark lean times, and we were only just into autumn. Truly, I wished them luck. I like trying different craft beers, and if I get to hear the brewery has become a producer, I will head back up for a taste. Maybe the same time next year - I needed to go back to St Fillans Golf Club with the Jimmy McFadyen Trophy and defend my title.

All in all, it was a very pleasant day. I headed off home.

There are a lot of things worse than getting stuck behind a slow driver on a winding road. I know that. It is just that it sometimes feels like the worst thing. One of my hobbies is to curse at drivers who slow to a stop at the least little bend in the road. Not today, though. I powered through the bends and promptly had to slow down again as I came up behind an old E registered Land Rover Defender. It was two tone with the lower half faded blue and the white upper half yellowed with the sun. The rear advertising said:

Mike McDougall
Painter & Decorator
Comrie
Tel: 832603

Who in this day and age doesn't put an area code or a mobile number on an advertisement?

All Creatures Great and Small was compulsory viewing when I was a lad and I was instantly transported back to the era of James Herriot and his books about his time as a vet in Yorkshire. The memory was further enhanced by a large Dalmatian dog sitting in the front passenger seat of the Land Rover as it bobbed its head back and forth, scouting for sheep no doubt. The Defender bumbled along with its over-inflated tyres, and I settled in behind it. There were no opportunities to overtake, but I didn't mind. It was just another pleasant way to pass the remains of the afternoon.

    I look forward to going back to St Fillans. I want to have a look at the fairy stone and enjoy a pint of whatever craft beer Arrans Loch Earn Brewery produces - with a bit o' luck.

Chapter four

DR MIDDLETON'S FREE INQUIRY INTO THE MIRACULOUS POWERS

Do I look like a robber?

I use the word 'robber' knowing it is wrong. What I should have asked you is, do I look like a housebreaker?

Theft by Housebreaking is the Scottish legal term for unlawful entry to a building. In England, they call it 'burglary,' Australians call it 'home invasions,' and Americans call it 'breaking and entering.' Some countries in the world give the crime the graphic title of 'violation of property,' which is quite a scary way to put it. However, almost everyone everywhere who finds their patio doors crow-barred open and their jewellery stolen, will call the police and say, 'there's been a robbery.'

Robbery has nothing to do with overcoming the security of a house. Robbery is defined as stealing property from someone by use of violence or threats of violence. Pointing a sawn-off shotgun at a bank teller and demanding money or taking a knife to someone's throat and threatening to kill them if they don't hand over their wallet. Nevertheless, people the world over still call the police and say, 'I've been robbed' to describe having had their house broken into and their property stolen.

To clarify, I don't look like a robber. I don't look like a housebreaker, a burglar or even a home violator. *Of course, I don't, you cretinous imbecile* (not you, the guy who mistook me for a robber).

Let me explain; I'm in my fifties, I have short grey hair and a bigger paunch than I would like. I spent thirty years as a police officer and if I learned anything it was good deportment - nipples leading, as they say. Looking the part is half the battle. So I walk like a police officer. I am unaware I walk like a police officer, it's not intentional. When I see fellow retired officers, I note they too have a tendency to walk head up, chest out, and hands clasped behinds their back. It is only then I check myself. I'll slow my pace and slouch a little, but it doesn't last long. Soon enough people will look at me and think, 'there's a policeman.'

I look even less like a robber when I am in the company of my wife and Monkeydog. I mean, who takes their middle-aged wife and mongrel along when breaking into a place? Thus, when the man came running out of his house intent on accusing my wife, my dog and I of being involved in some nefarious plot to rob him, I had to assume he was incredibly dim. But that is what happened when we went for a walk in Dunblane.

Dunblane is a town in Central Scotland about six miles north of Stirling, pleasantly situated on the north banks of the Allan Water. It is a commuter town, with a population of around 10,000, half of them are in the well off category, the other half obscenely rich. On average, Dunblane has the most expensive housing in Scotland because it doesn't have any areas of poor housing. Dunblane reeks of old money. It is a commuter town with good transport links to Glasgow and Edinburgh. Those in high paying city jobs like to get out of the grime and scuttle back to their quiet little town with its golf course, tennis club and idyllic setting.

Dunblane is famous for being the hometown of Scottish tennis hero Andy Murray and his brother Jamie. There is a golden post box at the roundabout on the High

Street, painted to commemorate Andy's 2012 Olympic gold medal when, at age twenty-five, he beat Roger Federer to win the men's singles title.

Andy Murray's journey started in Dunblane when he first swung a tennis racket at the age of three. By the time he was eight, he was competing with adults in a league. He turned professional in 2005, steadily climbed the rankings and by the time of the London 2012 Summer Olympics he had become so good journalists south of the border referred to him as British. (It is a peculiarity of the English media that those of us north of the border are referred to as Scottish when we lose and British when we win).

For all that we supported Murray to the hilt, we Scots still thought he would disappoint us with a last-minute 'clutch of defeat from the jaws of victory' - a pessimism drawn from our typical experience. This goes as far back as 1296 when, despite being garrisoned in the castle, our troops lost to the English at the Battle of Berwick. More recently we overwhelmingly voted to stay in Europe but still had Brexit forced upon us. Mostly though, our gloomy outlook has been instilled by our national football team.

Murray met Roger Federer in the final. Roger Federer, the greatest tennis player of this or any other era, an invincible giant of the game. Just four weeks earlier Federer had broken Murray in the Wimbledon men's final. Wimbledon was Federer's fifth title that year. It was his 7th Wimbledon title in all, his 17th Grand Slam title and 75th career title. They were to play the Olympic final in the same Wimbledon arena. The hopes and dreams of every English tennis fan rested on (the now British) Andy Murray. We cynical Scots are used to last-minute disillusionment, and our hopes and dreams remained with Murray not being so soundly thrashed that we couldn't show our peely-wally faces for a few weeks.

We were wrong. Andy Murray produced a sensational performance and visited near humiliation on Roger Federer. Murray took him apart with a performance of such magnitude that he pummelled Federer in straight sets 6-2, 6-1, 6-4 in under an hour. It was to be a wonderful summer; the Scots had no reason to hang their heads. Britain bathed in the glory of Murray's triumph and Scotland got a little colour on its cheeks.

As nice as Dunblane is, it is still remembered for the deadliest mass shooting in British history. On 13th March 1996 Thomas Hamilton, a former shopkeeper, armed with four handguns and hundreds of rounds of ammunition walked into Dunblane Primary School and shot at a class of five and six-year-olds. He killed sixteen children and one teacher before putting the gun to his own head. Both Andy and Jamie Murray were pupils of Dunblane Primary School and in the school at the time of the shooting. The effects of such a dreadfully evil act on the survivors are hard to fathom.

I was a police officer with Central Scotland Police back then. I was off duty when I heard the news. The shock and desperation were instant. Things like that don't happen in Scotland. We had had the Lockerbie Disaster in 1988, the horror of which had numbed me to the core. This murderous act was different. It was even more horrific and appalling because it was in my force area and only eight miles from where I lived and worked. On my return to duty, I got the job of high visibility patrol in Dunblane. The streets surrounding the primary school filled up with flowers and cuddly toys.

There wasn't a spare pavement near the school that didn't get carpeted with gifts from well-wishers. It was a sobering time. I read the notes attached to the bouquets of flowers. The heartfelt sorrow echoed in every word, and I stood there in full uniform and cried.

The tragedy had serious and wide-reaching implications. Public opinion had an enormous impact on the legislative changes that occurred because of the massacre. The Snowdrop Campaign, founded by families and friends of those affected by the tragedy, petitioned for a ban on private gun ownership and gained 750,000 signatures in a matter of weeks. The campaign stopped short of calling for a total ban on all guns. Instead, it appealed for all private ownership of handguns to be banned and those guns be held securely at authorised clubs. They weren't against recreational gun use; they were for sensible gun controls.

The combination of the public pressure and the anticipation of the findings of an official inquiry into Dunblane by Lord Cullen, caused a near-political crisis for the Conservative Government. The gun lobby looked out of touch and unsympathetic. Public pressure and the upcoming general election forced the government to pass legislation prohibiting all handguns above .22 calibre. Due to public and political pressure, the Government legislated far beyond the recommendations of the Cullen report. Although the report concluded the attack could not have been predicted, it raised serious questions about Hamilton's firearms licence. In my capacity as a police officer, I never hesitated in removing any person's firearms and questioning their suitability to hold a gun licence. If there was the slightest concern, I'd take all their weapons and ammunition. Dunblane was always my consideration at the back of these decisions.

The legislation passed after Dunblane resulted in the UK having some of the strictest gun laws in the world. Since then Scotland has had no further mass shootings. If it were up to me, I'd make the laws even stricter. I see compelling evidence that countries which have strict gun laws have little or no mass shootings.

If there were any more argument required, it is the story behind the death of an Idaho woman in a Walmart. The woman and her husband loved everything about guns. They practised at shooting ranges. They hunted and both had permits to carry concealed firearms. Her husband gave her a present for her Christmas one year that he hoped would make her life more comfortable: a purse with a special pocket for a concealed weapon.

The day after Christmas, she took her new gift on a trip with her husband and her two-year-old son. They arrived at a Walmart store. In the back, near the electronics section, she left her purse unattended for a moment. The inquisitive two-year-old son reached into the purse, unzipped the compartment, found the gun and shot his mother in the head. The sad part is the husband is angry. He is angry that people use the story to grand stand on gun rights. I just don't get it. How could anyone be part of such a tragic circumstance and still support the wide availability of guns?

The tendency is to concentrate on homicides; it makes better news headlines. Did you know over sixty percent of gun deaths are suicides? It is the second most common cause of death amongst Americans aged between 15 - 34. Guns are convenient and lethal. Studies prove you can substantially reduce the suicide rate by limiting access to guns. Guns are like dildos in this respect; the lonelier the owner is, the more likely they are to get used.

Many years ago, Dunblane sat astride the road north. Now there is a by-pass, and it is easy to avoid. There is no need to pop into Dunblane unless you live there or are a tennis fan. If you take the main road through Dunblane, without turning off, you will only see an M&S food hall, a brief glimpse of Dunblane Hydro and pass the gates to Queen Victoria School. Thus, I recommend turning left down the narrow High Street, at the end of which you will see Murray's commemorative golden post box. Until the arrival of the golden post box Dunblane was principally notable for its Cathedral.

Dunblane Cathedral is breathtaking; it is almost the length of a football pitch. The sheer scope in such a small place is a surprise, considering Stirling, with a population over ten times as much as Dunblane, has no cathedral. It is as impressive as any of Historic Scotland's buildings since it is they, not the Church who look after it. Inside it is just as impressive. The nave walls are more weathered on the inside than out. That's because for over three hundred years it stood without a roof. A spiral staircase at the West wall leads to a viewing platform where you can take in all the grandeur and see the full beauty of the stained glass windows that cascade sunlight into the apse. In the 1980s a Dutch company installed two hundred and eight organ pipes, requiring the makers to pop across from Holland once every year to tune them up. The pipes scale the north-east wall like soldiers standing to attention. Gleaming woodwork and stone carvings catch interest, enough to while away half an hour. The pews are carved with every native Scottish plant and animal - a great place to explore and contemplate. In out of the rain, I'd happily sit for an hour soaking up the atmosphere and thinking my own thoughts.

At the far side of the Cathedral is a small car park. We abandoned the car and took Monkeydog a walk down by the river. The roadway descends to a traffic-free footpath; it ducks under the railway line and past the Faery Bridge before opening out to a large grassy area which houses a football pitch and a play park. We sat on the swings; then I popped Monkeydog onto the chute which cascades in three separate sections down a steep hill. Monkeydog wasn't so sure at first but he gamely came bounding back up the steps wagging his tail. I thought he wanted another go; he had different ideas and avoided my clutches until we had made our way back down the steps. He is a smart dog.

Behind the play park is a strange piece of rolling land, surrounded on three sides by the River Allan. The land is covered in ferns, through which there are many well-trodden paths. We followed the river then had to climb a steep hill where at the top, breathless; we stopped to admire the view. We wound our way through the ferns until, surprise; the land flattened out, and in the middle of it all we came across another football field. A flat and manicured pitch, thus well used. Yet, I noted there were only goalposts at one end. I wondered if the other set had been whisked away in the middle of the night. *Who would steal a single goalpost?* I imagined a team of footballers sneaking down there at night in their black and white hooped tops and making off with them over their shoulders. I don't know; it seemed strange.

We explored further and followed the path to a bridge that crossed the railway line. The crossing is one of only two entrances to this piece of land, neither of which supports vehicular traffic, saving it from being developed into housing.

On the other side of the railway line, we found ourselves lost. There were several paths from which to choose. The path we picked brought us out in Ramoyle. Ramoyle is a quaint part of Dunblane only two hundred yards long. It comprises one narrow street. On either side are dainty cottages with lovely names; Pear Tree Cottage, Ashentree, Lavender Cottage, to name but a few.

There is a sign halfway up one building to keep an eye out for; this provides information on how Ramoyle got its name. It tells how the narrow street, at one time, was the main road into the town from the north. Many of the existing houses date from the 17th and 18th centuries, occupied originally by handloom weavers.

As we sauntered along, we came across an elderly, well-to-do gentleman who was renovating a cottage. A wiry man who I put in his seventies. He didn't strike me as being short of a shilling or two. I suspect he was renovating one of his properties in readiness to rent. He gave us a big cheery smile, happy to take a breather when I engaged him in conversation.

"Excuse me, can you tell me which direction it is to Dunblane Cathedral?"

"Straight down that road," he pointed to his left, "you can't miss it."

"Thank you."

"Where are you from," he asked.

"Alloa direction."

"Alloa, I think I have only been there once," conveying the meaning, but without actually saying, 'once was enough,' before adding, "Alloa used to have the biggest gin distillery in the world."

The biggest gin distillery in the world - this was news. I was born and brought up in Alloa and recall we once had a thriving beer industry. Alloa Ales were famous the world over, but I hadn't heard of a gin distillery, far less the largest in the world.

"Whereabouts?" I enquired.

"At Kennetpans."

Kennetpans is a tiny wee place on the other side of Clackmannan, the capital of Scotland's smallest county. I was sure there is nothing there that could once have been a gin distillery.

"Are you sure? There is nothing much in Kennetpans now."

"Oh! It is just an old ruin."

Something in my brain clicked.

"Are you talking about the overgrown ruins seen from the new Clackmannanshire Bridge?"

I had often wondered about that place.

Our spritely renovator enlightened me.

"Yes, that's the place. Way back it was the largest gin distillers in the world. At one time it supplied all of London with gin. The hill beside it is made up of the ballast of ships, mainly from Holland, dropping off counterweight to make way for the gin. They later made whisky, I believe. And it was the cheapest sort."

I did not know that. It was something I would have to investigate. I made a mental note to plan a future walk there with Monkeydog. The information you can learn when you get out and about on foot and talk to people is just great, isn't it?

We continued our leisurely walk back towards the Cathedral. We stopped to admire the beautiful gardens of a large corner plot. The rear garden rose at the sides like an amphitheatre, splendid colourful rockeries sat on all sides looking down to a comfortable set of wicker chairs. As we ambled around to the front of the house, we saw the owner, another elderly gentleman, on his hands and knees plucking at his lawn. He was a tad plumpish but all the jollier for it. I expressed my admiration for his hard work on his garden. Enthusiastically he regaled us with tales of his mossy grass and how it was growing longer into the year than at any time in the past. His underlying accusation that global warming was to blame.

Further on we saw a similar information sign to the one we had seen in Ramoyle. This sign told us we were now in 'Braeport.' As far as I could tell we were on the same street and only about one hundred yards further along. Braeport or *'the gate on the hill'* was the town's northern gateway where traders paid their tolls on market days. The adjoining barn was where tenants deposited their annual tithes to the bishop.

Rather than head home, we continued past the cathedral towards High Street. There was a foldaway sign at the bottom of an external staircase advertising the *'Leighton Library,'* the oldest purpose-built library in Scotland dating back to 1684. Mrs McEwan went on with Monkeydog in search of a coffee and I stopped to have a look. I climbed the steps and entered. The library is a single room, the length of the walls taken up with wooden bookcases which housed ancient tomes. An elderly couple stood at a desk near the entrance and welcomed me in with enthusiastic smiles.

"Good day, welcome to the Leighton Library."

"Hello," I replied looking around in amazement at all the leather-clad books on display.

"Would you like some information about the library?" the grey-haired lady asked.

"Yes. Yes, I would, thank you."

"Do you know anything about Robert Leighton?"

"No. I have never heard of him."

"Ah well, Robert Leighton was the Bishop of Dunblane for many years in the seventeenth century before becoming the Archbishop of Glasgow. He was a lover of books, and he built up a collection throughout his life. When he died, he bequeathed his money to build this library, and he had his entire collection of 1400 books moved from his retiral home in Sussex to here. The books had to be transported by horse and cart and by sea. The original presses to the left house all his books. These have been added to over the years, and now we have around 4,500 volumes printed in eighty-nine languages. Feel free to take a look around."

I ambled through the library wondering what weighty knowledge these books held, seeing if anything caught my attention.

"I presume we are not allowed to handle these books?" I asked.

"Yes, you can. If you want to look at one we will be happy to take it out for you. You can read it there," she pointed at a reading desk in the middle of the library which bore two cushions, presumably where they laid the books.

I stopped at a large leather-bound book edged in gold leaf; it was dull and worn. *'Dr Middleton's Free Inquiry into the Miraculous Powers'* was the title. For centuries it had sat, unopened, waiting for me to come along and garner the secrets within.

"That looks interesting," I said to the librarian.

"Would you like me to take it out so you can have a look?" She asked.

"No point. I haven't got my glasses."

"Perhaps you would like to come back another time?"

"Yes, I'd like that. When are you open?"

"We only open between 11 a.m. and 1 p.m., May to September and only Monday to Saturday."

She could see I was puzzled by the unusually short opening hours.

"We are volunteers, you see."

"Well, you are doing a commendable job. I will come back another day. Next time I will make sure I bring my glasses."

I headed out to join my wife and Monkeydog, wondering what miraculous powers I might learn on my return.

I have since been back to the library and read many remarkable things. I am impressed by the genuine interest the volunteers take in their visitors. They are elderly in body but sharp of mind. Once I sat for an hour reading Hugh Blair's *Lectures on Rhetoric* but mostly listening to the two gentlemen volunteers as they traded their knowledge of the authors on display. They gasped in awe and wonder at each tome they took from the shelves. I listened as they serenaded a young lady visitor with their eloquence, politely massaging her mind with curious attention. Learning where she was from, who she was and what value she gave to the world. Their enquiries were florid and full of praise, amusing and persuasive. They spoke from the heart leaving a deep and long impression of their strong and lively imagination.

In due course the two gentlemen got me talking, and they astutely guided me from one topic to another. Each caller is invited to record their name in the visitor book, tell others of the place and encouraged to return. I signed the book and promised to include the details of the library in this book. Leighton's Library, I can assure the reader, is worth a visit just to soak up the enthusiasm of the volunteers.

Down from Leighton's Library, Dunblane's narrow High Street has some nice little shops selling ornaments, knick-knacks and gewgaws. The aptly named 'Old Curiosity Shop,' for example, selling all sorts of gaudy crockery that might once have adorned my great grandmother's mantelpiece. High Street also has some nice coffee shops. Mrs McEwan and Monkeydog had settled on an outside table at Choices Delicatessen where the pavement is narrow. I had to keep pulling Monkeydog under the table to let pedestrians get past with their prams. Not quite the relaxing place you might find in France or Italy. The coffee and sandwiches took their time to appear, but as a result, they were even more satisfying. The choice on offer is varied and the portions plentiful.

On our way back to the car we spotted an impressive stone built cottage. It had a gated archway at the front and looked to be under renovation. Through the gate we could see a square courtyard that served as a lovely private space. On the left side of the cottage, a large arched window allowed us to see inside to a gloriously sized room.

To the right of the gated entrance, a low wall was all that separated us from the kitchen window. A handwritten card sat in the window displaying a mobile phone number, 'If no-one is in please call...' it said. I surmised the building was up for sale. Mrs McEwan's natural nosiness took over. Before I knew it, she was on the other side of the wall. Monkeydog jumped over and followed. It did not look like anyone was home; I trailed behind, wary of trespassing. A cat stared at us from a window ledge. A sign of occupancy? We rounded the back of the building and walked up the driveway. The driveway was empty of cars, which reassured me the place was as vacant as it looked. At the back of the house we came to a small, easy to maintain garden. Good, I hate gardening. My first property was a second-floor flat and had two window boxes - I paved them over.

Mrs McEwan seemed interested; she gave me one of her smiles that said, 'I like this place, can we buy it?' I scrunched up my nose in reply as I contemplated the cost. Then a shout broke my train of thought.

"What the hell are you doing in my garden," an angry man in paint-stained overalls appeared at the back of us.

"We were just having a look," my wife explained as she about turned and sidled past him retracing her steps towards the driveway. Monkeydog followed with his tail between its legs.

"Are you trying to rob the effing place?" He screamed, veins popping in his neck. He looked at me like I had just run over his cat and disposed of its remains in a trash can. I noticed his fists gripped tight by his side.

I considered my position. Under normal circumstances, I might have put on my posh voice and expressed my interest in buying the property. I could have kept it going for weeks, batting phone calls back and forth promising I was putting the finances together, then spectacularly letting the oaf down. Nothing less than he deserved. Shouting at us like that, I mean really! Okay, we were in his back garden, but we were obviously not there to rob the place. It also wasn't the right moment for me to go into a detailed lesson on the definition of robbery either. A civil, 'Can I help you?' was all he required. He didn't need to go blasting off with both barrels. Who the hell did he think he was?

"I don't expect to have to have people effing wandering about my back garden when I am effing working," still livid.

That was it for me. Enough already. I didn't say a word, returning his stare I walked back up the path and edged my way past him, never taking my eyes off his. Not that I wasn't a little worried about being assaulted, I just didn't show it. Giving him the impression I could handle him. I'd already decided his property, as nice as it would be, was beyond my fiscal capacity. So I continued to look back at him as I walked off his property. A brilliant piece of mischief came to mind, I couldn't help myself. I made no effort to placate the angry man, I made no excuses. He found us in his back garden, and I walked past him without saying a word. Then, about ten yards away from him, I shouted, "Run. Quick run!"

My wife, and I took off down the hill at a sprint, struggling to hold in our giggles. Monkeydog skipped along beside us as if it were his favourite thing. A story we would later relate with glee.

Chapter five

I CAN SEE ELVIS FROM HERE

You can buy a two-bedroom semi-detached house with a small garden in the village of Coalsnaughton for around eighty thousand pounds. As you will imagine, there is a reason for this; there isn't very much in Coalsnaughton to commend it. *Wikipedia* has a one-line entry for the town: *'Coalsnaughton is a village in Clackmannanshire, Scotland - just south of Tillicoultry'.* That's it. Short, uninformative but none-the-less accurate. A village summed up by its position to another unremarkable town.

As a police officer, I had reasons to travel to Coalsnaughton. Just like any other town it was subject to drunken behaviour and occasionally people called us to deal with the disturbance. Because of a story related to me by a respected colleague, I was much more wary when attending calls to Coalsnaughton.

One night, many moons ago, a man with a murderous purpose went to the Coalsnaughton Burns Club armed with an axe. The would be assassin approached the committee member on the door, raised the axe above his head and screamed his intention to kill him. The doorman backed away in fear for his life, followed by the axe wielding would-be-killer. In the lounge all eyes turned to the axeman. As he backed away, the committee member tripped and fell to the floor, landing between the fixed seats and a table. With all the force he could muster, the would-be-killer swung the axe at the desperate man on the floor. Fortunately, the axe missed its target and buried itself in the heavy wooden table; the blade disappeared so far into the oak only a tiny sliver of the blade remained in view. And there it remained, he tugged at it with all his strength but no amount of hernia inducing exertion could magic this axe from the table. Immovable like Excalibur in stone.

Sezing the opportunity, a group of men, emboldened by a couple of pints and a few whiskies, pounced on the axeman, wrestled him to the ground and held him there until the police arrived and took him away.

Coalsnaughton Burns Club was set up to do nothing more than celebrate the Scottish Bard. Our very own Rabbie Burns, a man given more to romance than violence. I picture he turned in his grave.

My colleague's first job as a police officer was to return the heavy wooden table to the Coalsnaughton Burns Club after its appearance in court, where it had been exhibit number one. With his tutor they manhandled the table into a big van. Unable to shut the door, my colleague had to sit in the rear and hold on to the table as his tutor drove the van to the club. There they extricated the table and shuffled it back into the lounge where the secretary signed for it. The axe still remained sticking out of the table as a salutary warning to all.

As a police officer, I had many a reason to go to Coalsnaughton. I was never sure what would greet me, so I was always wary.

As a tourist, there is only one reason to travel to Coalsnaughton, that being the *Muircot Farmshop*. To get there travel east from Stirling and follow the signs for the B9140. Drive into Coalsnaughton and out again, Muircot Farmshop is on the left as you leave.

Muircot Farmshop is more of a restaurant than a shop. While it has the usual array of homemade jams, chutneys and the like, it is not the place to do your weekly shop. Similar to most places of its ilk, prices for the jams and chutneys can catch you unawares. All the price stickers are on the back of the jars, so you need to lift them up and turn them around to have your breath taken away. I always make a purchase. I know it is indulgent and it might be psychological, but these overpriced preserves just taste better.

Moving through to the restaurant, what struck me first was the outlook. The back of the building is wall to wall glass giving unobstructed views of the Ochil Hills. A fine backdrop to the Wee County. The morning I visited a low cloud swept eastward caressing the top of the hills. I ordered breakfast, sat by the window and looked to see if I could glimpse Elvis.

Ben Cleuch above Tillicoultry is the Ochil's highest hill at 721 metres, yet the ascent is easy. The beautiful Tillicoultry Glen has an excellent path following Daiglen Burn to the foot of the upper slope where the summit awaits. Ben Cleuch is also the easiest of the hills in the Ochils to identify. It sits above a quarry and, at certain times of the year, the moss forms a picture of Elvis playing his guitar. (For those of you who haven't heard of him, Elvis was a popular American singer known for his lyrical voice and gyratory hips, maybe not as famous as that Scots guy... what's his name? You know, the one who invented the telephone). Okay, you might have to squint your eyes, and it is not until someone points it out to you that you notice Elvis, but once you see Elvis, you always see Elvis. The moss lightens and darkens throughout the year, so the picture it paints changes. It is like taking the *Rorschach Ink Blot Test.*

Psychologists use the *Rorschach Inkblot Test* to determine the personality characteristics and emotional functioning of their patients. I wonder what underlying disorder seeing Elvis identifies? You are all shook up? You have a suspicious mind? You have a little less conversation?

I was first told about Elvis on the hill by an old police colleague, PC Barbeque Bill. We were on general patrol driving towards Tillicoultry.

"I can see Elvis from here," said Bill as he stared out the passenger window.

"What are you talking about?"

"Elvis on Ben Cleuch."

I scrunched up my face. "Elvis on Ben Cleuch?"

"Yeah, Elvis on Ben Cleuch."

I glanced up at the hill.

"Still don't know what you are talking about," and went back to concentrating on the road.

"Stop the car."

So I did. I stopped the car.

"Now look at the moss. It looks like Elvis."

"Where?"

"Right above the quarry."

And then it took shape. The human brain likes to organise patterns into recognisable forms. It is why we perceive animals or other objects in cloud formations or we see the face of the 'Man in the Moon'. Our unconscious brain tries to make sense of random shapes, an early warning system for our survival instinct. Is that a tiger in the woods? Is that an angry face of a man who will attack me? Thus, the moss above the quarry formed of a silhouette of Elvis in my mind. The power of suggestion at work.

"Yeah, I see it now," I confirmed, "but that doesn't look like a guitar he is holding.

PC Barbeque Bill gave me a withering look, "you disgust me at times," he said.

"Why, you a mind-reader now?"

Ever since having Elvis pointed out I have looked for other rock stars in the hills. Once I saw Jimi Hendrix, halfway up Dumyat - but he was playing the flute, so that didn't quite work. There are also some trees between Alva and Tillicoultry that look like an upside down head and torso. Macabre.

In no time at all, my poached eggs on brown toast arrived, and they were pretty delicious. As was the cappuccino - they didn't skimp on the chocolate sprinkle which entirely covered the froth. My nose required attention from my napkin after every sip. The seeded bread came toasted the colour of gold, perfect. I liked that my poached eggs didn't run away but were still moist. It was a nice change to a bacon roll.

The restaurant only serves breakfast until 11:30 a.m. and lunch, according to the menu, doesn't start until noon. I'm not sure what they do in the half hour gap. Lunch also stops getting served at 3 p.m., but last orders aren't until 4:30 p.m. There is a wonderful selection of cakes to choose from up by the counter, so I dare say no-one will go hungry. The coffee is particularly fine for washing down a slice of carrot cake.

As I sat admiring the view, grey clouds padded their way across the hills giving out a constant drizzle - Thomas

Hardy weather, notice given of an encroaching winter. Patches of moss darkened the upper reaches of Ben Cleuch and disappeared into the greyness. Further along, towards Alva, emerald green trees blanketed half the slope. As it flattened out towards the bottom, the darkness of the emerald green gave way to the much lighter lush grass on which you could play crown green bowls, it seemed.

The conurbation of Tillicoultry spread out below me looking silent and empty. The artificial ski slope cut into the hill. Firpark Ski Centre keeps itself busy of an evening, only letting up in the summer months. I religiously conveyed two of my sons there every Monday night for many years. They both passed successive grades up to instructor level. Now they love sliding with style and have a taste for expensive winter ski holidays; Dad, unfortunately, remains at home.

I was always in awe of their skill, how they could thunder down a slope at seventy miles per hour on a crash course with me at the bottom where I stood shivering with cold and fear. At the last moment, they would flick their legs to the side and slither the last few feet sideways stopping inches from my cowering body. I felt a strange mixture of irritation and pride.

Inevitably, as I sat reminiscing, the rain came on heavier. A turmoil of darker clouds rolled in from the west. The steady drizzle became a rapid free fall. There was no sign of a let up. Several couples stood by the door pulling the collars up on their coats in readiness for a dash to their cars. I stayed where I was, happy to order another coffee and watch the rain bounce off the wooden picnic table on the other side of the glass, sending me into a hypnotic state. Scotland may be the most beautiful country in the world, even from a small characterless ex-mining village, but if you aren't happy to sit inside drinking coffee, then make sure you bring a raincoat and a brolly.

Chapter six

WELL JUST LOOK AT THE VIEWS

I shall always remember the first time I saw Craiglockhart Campus of Edinburgh Napier University. It is an impressive Italian style stone building. It sits on well kept grounds overlooking Edinburgh and has Wester Craiglockhart Hill as a backdrop. Originally built as a Hydrotherapy Treatment Centre by the Craiglockhart Hydropathic Company in the late 1800's, (if this ever comes up in a pub quiz you are going to thank me) it is an imposing structure commanding the higher ground in about fifteen acres of land.

Hydrotherapy is the use of water to treat different physical conditions, like arthritis and rheumatic complaints. I presume they had warm pools for exercising away the aches and pains of the patients. A whole lot more effective than homoeopathy, which is proven to be a load of nonsense. Water is also a superb treatment for dehydration; I can knowledgeably impart.

It makes sense. Exercise is very much underrated for its health benefits. If you were to read an article in a newspaper that declared a miracle new cure for cancer, heart attacks, rheumatoid arthritis, ankylosing spondylitis (or whatever you suffer from) you would read with interest. You might be surprised to find out the miracle cure is not a magic tablet or a new potion. It is getting off your backside - the thing we call exercise. Multiple studies show that exercise improves physical function and health related quality of life for almost every medical complaint there is. Everything from chronic obstructive pulmonary disease to depression. The only thing I haven't read it cures is warts, but you never know.

During the First World War, the War Cabinet commandeered the Craiglockhart building for use as a military psychiatric hospital to treat shell-shocked officers. The poets Siegfried Sassoon and Wilfred Owen were patients during that time. Sassoon was parcelled off to Craiglockhart in response to an anti-war letter he wrote - *not much wrong with him then*. In his semi-autobiographical novel, *Sherston's Progress*, he describes his sessions with the doctor as a *'friendly confabulation'* of an evening.

One evening I asked whether he thought I was suffering from shell-shock.
'Certainly not,' he replied.
'What have I got then?'
'Well, you appear to be suffering from an anti-war complex.'

The doctor was an army psychiatrist called William Rivers, born, to the day, one hundred years before your narrator. From all accounts, Rivers was a compassionate man who tolerated the anti-war sentiment of Sassoon with sympathy. On the one hand, his job was to nurse his patients back to reasonable mental health, but he also knew in doing so it would be their duty to return to the peril of the front-line.

Sassoon illustrates a session with him; *I went along to Rivers' room to give my anti-war complex an airing.* Which must have been a brave thing to do. He knew deserters could be shot and cowards vilified. William Rivers offered no recrimination of such a standpoint. Instead, Sassoon was allowed to send off a letter to his Aunt Evelyn requesting his golf clubs. They arrived the next day, sped up by the three labels, all inscribed 'urgent'. Soon he was slicing his tee-shots into the long grass of the nearest golf course. No wonder he described his psychiatrist as a *great and good man who gave me friendship and guidance.'*

It was at Craiglockhart that Wilfred Owen found himself influenced by Sassoon. His poetry, in stark contrast to the general perception of the conflict, described the awful dreadfulness of trench warfare. He witnessed his fellow soldiers 'floundering' as they tried to put on their gas masks when poison seeped towards them and saw many more horrors. His war was one long traumatic experience. Diagnosed with shell shock, they sent him to Craiglockhart for treatment. Although Owen could have legitimately spent the rest of the war years on home-duty in a Northern Command Depot, he decided to return to active service in France. It is speculation, but his decision to return to the front-line is thought to have been a result of Sassoon being sent back from the war after receiving a bullet to the head. Apparently, his non-fatal injury resulted from friendly fire. In an uncharitable thought, I wondered if it was self-inflicted friendly fire.

Wilfred Owen made his way back to the fighting without the knowledge of Sassoon who said he would 'stab him in the leg' if he were even to contemplate it. It would have been preferable to the fate that awaited him. He returned to the front-line in August 1918. In October that year he earned the Military Cross for courage and leadership when storming enemy strongholds near the village of Joncourt.

One week before Armistice (4th November 1918), Owen was killed when his unit advanced across the Sambre-Oise Canal.

As the church bells sounded across Britain, ringing out in celebration of the end of the war, Wilfred Owen's family received the telegram informing them of his death.

- O what fatuous sunbeams toil
To break earth's sleep at all.

(Last two lines of *Futility* by Wilfred Owen)

Which is almost as good as Lee Mack's ode entitled *Old Women's Knickers.*

Roses are red
Violets are blue
Ethel's are green.

After the war Craiglockhart served as a convent and a Catholic teacher training college before becoming Napier College then Napier Polytechnic and is now part of Edinburgh Napier University.

I was there to drop off number two son, who was starting his fourth year studying business and entrepreneurship. There was a large 'Welcome' sign on the grass bank at the entrance. Colourful, three foot-high, plastic letters.

"See what I did for you, Dad?"

"What?"

"I knew you would drop me off today, so I arranged for the welcome sign to be out," he smiled.

I suppose it was quite entrepreneurial of him. Taking credit for something he didn't do shows a flair for capitalising on a situation.

Above the sign is the extensive new wing, built to house the business school. A silver curved lecture room juts out like a large glass eye. It conjured up an image of an alien spaceship reversed into the building, strategically placed to keep an eye on the capital. It contrasts with the old Italian style architecture, but I think it works. Combining the new and spectacular with the old and fortified. A fitting thing for a university. It is an iconic part of the student life there.

I first caught sight of the strange appendage when number two son was about twelve. I had taken him to play in a junior golf open at *The Merchants of Edinburgh Golf Course*. A course designed by Ben Sayers in 1907. It is likely to be the course Siegfried Sassoon sliced his way around with the clubs sent to him by his aunt. It sits on and behind Craiglockhart Hill and at one point takes you to the top of the Wester. From there number two son and I marvelled at the silver bullet spaceship projecting out of the Craiglockhart building. We didn't have a clue what it was at that time.

It was a good day that day, number two son enjoyed his golf. The Merchants of Edinburgh is a short par sixty-five course, which allows for a straight hitting twelve-year-old to score well. I was always keen to return to it and either play it or have number three son enter their junior open, but never quite managed. I wondered if it was one of the reasons number two son went to the Napier Open Day. Perhaps he had the notion of playing golf from time to time, not realising his studies would keep him too busy.

The Open Day at Craiglockhart campus was the deciding factor in his choice. We sauntered amiably around the building, but it wasn't until we entered the spaceship, a fully functioning lecture theatre, that we were blown away. The full-length glass eye gives a view right across Edinburgh to the estuary of the River Forth where you can identify each of the three crossings. We were further smitten with the enthusiasm of the lecturer, Professor Stephen Robertson, who talked in an unrestrained and excited manner about his fellow colleagues and the business course. His final summation was enough to seal number two son's destiny for the next four years.

'So, potential students, we have the most remarkable and passionate lecturers. We have the right materials, and we have the right instruction. If you decide to embark on this course of study, I can promise you one thing. If you listen and learn, you can never enter a coffee shop again without being able to put your finger on what is right or wrong. When they get it right, you will appreciate it. When they get it wrong, which is most of the time, you will be deeply frustrated. It is the curse of knowledge. If you don't want damned with this knowledge, then you should leave now.'

Professor Robertson turned to look out of the glass eye for a few seconds then turned back to our gathering and added, *'Or, you could just ignore everything and look at the views'.*

I bade number two son farewell and headed off to Mortonhall Golf Course, to play an old friend. The road carves its way through the Merchants of Edinburgh course, igneous rock towering above me on the one side.

Mortonhall Golf Course was only a mile away, and I arrived early enough to have a leisurely coffee in the clubhouse. The door entry system required me to press a buzzer and wait. I did but a cleaner let me in before the voice on the speaker system was able to ask what I wanted or who I was. The clubhouse is decorated in wood and the bar is inviting. I entered and found it empty.

I crossed to the bar counter. An apple shaped lady with black hair, black blouse and black leggings emerged from a room at the back to berate me. She pointed at the speaker system next to the gantry; connected to the buzzer at the door.

"You need to give me time to answer it," her voice filled with admonition.

"Oh, I'm sorry," I replied in as placatory a manner as I could, "the cleaner let me in."

"You don't need to keep pressing it. I have to get from there to here before I can pick it up."

I nodded in agreement, hoping we could move on and I could order my coffee.

"You only need to press it once. Pressing it twice won't get me to open it any quicker."

I only pressed it the once. What was I meant to do when the cleaner opened the door for me? I nodded at her again, feigning obedience.

"It takes a few seconds for me to get to it you know?"

Now she had me irritated. I pictured myself persuading her to follow me outside on some ruse, then as she stepped outside I'd shut the door on her. Let her stand there and press the buzzer; see how she liked it.

Instead I apologised again. I needed coffee.

"I'm sorry, I was just looking for a coffee."

I imagined her standing outside pressing the buzzer to get back in and me crawling over to the speaker phone at

69

the pace of a snail - which would still have been quicker than her.

"Well, you only need to press it once, then you have to wait for me to answer it. I'm not Usain Bolt, you know."

Usian Bolt? A sloth has more get up and go than you. The only way you would brighten a room is if you walked away from the window.

"You just need to press it once. Keeping your finger on it won't get me to open it any quicker."

Yes, I know, you told me. I was almost ready to walk out, find myself a shop up the road and settle for a can of Irn Bru.

"What kind of coffee do you want?"

"A cappuccino please."

At last, she stopped moaning about the stupid buzzer and served me.

"That will be £2.50," she said before making any effort in any direction to start the coffee brewing process. I wonder if she sensed I was miffed and ready to walk out. If she sensed that, then she was correct. I was even more miffed now - £2.50 for a cup of coffee!

I rummaged in my wallet and handed over three pound coins.

"Have you not got fifty pence?" she said rolling her eyes as if I had committed the capital crime of failing to have the right change.

"No, it's all I have," before adding, "you keep the change."

I was quick to offer up extra the 50p as a tip, but only because I didn't want to be supping on a cappuccino laced with spittle. The coffee went from expensive to extortion.

"I'll bring it over to you," she said.

I sat near the bar, hoping the coffee wouldn't be cold by the time it made it to my table. A few minutes later the apple shaped barmaid placed a frothy cup of coffee in front of me. It tasted good whether or not it had extra ingredients. I sipped the coffee as my eyes drank in the view down the 18th fairway.

Mortonhall Golf Course is splendid. It has some spectacular views. You wouldn't think you were in the middle of Scotland's capital. The lay of the land protects players from the noise of the city. My favourite hole is the 17th which is a picturesque par three that skirts with the danger of a pond to the left and a green that slopes towards you. The incline helps hold your tee shot but leaves you in danger of a three putt if you are not careful. I wasn't careful.

Even so, I had a pleasant round of golf, it was a nice, warm and sunny day for September. The course was so quiet that if we hadn't passed a couple of old codgers on the back nine, I would have thought we had the course to ourselves. Round complete we had a quick drink at the bar, a much more reasonably priced orange and soda water. The barmaid had also thawed to a chill.

When it was time to leave, I took my glass back up to the counter to save the barmaid having to collect it from the table. She watched me do this but offered no thanks. When I got to the main door, I looked back at the bar and saw she had disappeared through the back. I held my finger on the buzzer and could hear its irritating persistent ring. The barmaid appeared from the back and grabbed the speaker phone. Only then did I stop pressing it, ducked down and ran away.

Chapter seven

HERCULES

It might have been a rubbish place for a battlefield but as a playground Sheriffmuir is hard to top. Sheriffmuir lies on the slopes of the Ochil Hills which form a stunning backdrop to Clackmannanshire (The Wee County). Three roads converge at The Sheriffmuir Inn, a 17th-century country pub. It is at the Dunblane side of the Ochil Hills, but it feels like you are in the heart of the Ochils. Each road involves a fair climb, yet there are always Lycra-clad cyclists powering their way up the single track roads. If driving, you might have to sit behind one for a while before they pull in and let you pass. On the way down many suddenly appear behind you, freewheeling at speed, putting all that stored energy to use. An hour to the top and ten minutes down.

The north side of the Ochils has a road just off the A9 at Blackford that has a gentler incline. It is still impossibly hard for the average bike commuter to power up all the way. That requires the legs of Bradley Wiggins and no little perseverance. You might want to take a breather at Sheriffmuir's Atlantic Wall.

The Atlantic wall was the name given to a massive coastal defensive structure built on Hitler's orders, stretching all the way from Norway, along the Belgium and French coastline, to the Spanish border. The wall was built to repulse an Allied attack on Nazi-occupied Europe – wherever it was planned for. So we built a reinforced concrete mock-up of the wall on Sheriffmuir and used it to train soldiers to assault fortified areas. What remains are concrete blocks peppered with bullet holes and shell blasts offering a glimpse of the damage the weaponry of the time was capable of.

The road going south from the Sheriffmuir Inn winds its way around the back of Dumyat where there is parking for those wishing to walk to the top of the rocky mound. Walking up to the top of Dumyat from this side is the sensible thing to do, but I would recommend sturdy boots. Plimsolls might get you there, but not without a twisted ankle or a blister or two.

Dumyat is worth the climb.   I can't help but stop on the way up and admire the views. If the weather is favourable, the panorama is a delight. It is an incredible sight looking down on Wallace's Monument and across to Stirling Castle. You can see the River Forth as it meanders through the Wee County creating a natural border with the rest of the world. At the summit, the view extends north to the Highland Boundary Fault, west to Ben Lomond and east to the Pentland Hills behind Edinburgh. On a clear day you can see Edinburgh Castle sitting proud above the three Forth crossings.

The Dumyat Memorial, a cairn with a slatted metal brazier, sits at the peak. Once a year, Ochil Hills Mountain Rescue Team take up wood and coal to light it on Hogmanay. It would be nice to have it burning through the winter but lugging fuel to the top is a hell of a job.

I tried, and failed, to make it a habit for my family to climb to the top of Dumyat on New Years Day. The first time we did it Mrs McEwan got halfway up before she complained of asthma. The kids bounded on crunching their boots on the frosty ground and enjoyed a healthy dose of dopamine from the exercise. I snapped a few pictures and wished all my friends a Happy New Year from the top - via text. The 'I did it' sensation plummeted in line with our core temperature. The biting wind freezing the sweat on our backs. A minute later we were on our way back down to escape the sub-zero chill. The lack of shelter (and WiFi) scuppered future enthusiasm.

Number three son came up with a business idea to sell coffee at the top. The summit is busy on New Year's day. I know he would have made a some cash. However, transporting the required equipment and fresh water up to the top would have been a logistical nightmare. Also the frostbite wouldn't be worth the effort.

There is a group who make it a New Year tradition to be at the top of Dumyat for the sunrise. They wake in the dark put on their walking boots and climb to the top. When I worked the night shift, I might see their torches flashing across the hillside like light sabres. I hankered to be up there with them. I think it would be a marvellous experience, but I had to work. I worked a lot of night shifts in my career and I always felt privileged to be awake when the sun came up. Witnessing the first rays of sun from the top of Dumyat seems such a divine way of bringing in each new year.

Come dawn on a quiet nightshift, I would take a drive to the Ditch Farm road end at the west end of Tullibody. From there I could see the full range of the splendid Ochil Hills, all the way from Muckhart to Stirling. The fault climbs virtually from sea level to 1600 feet in less than a few hundred metres and the hills behind rise again to over 2000 feet, a more appropriate name would be the 'Ochil Mountains'. As daylight approached I'd see the sun flash across the sky igniting every cloud with the most beautiful display of reds, scarlet, and orange. I'd often prolong my knocking off time to see the dawn break and the sun flood across the splurge of yellow rapeseed fields that carpeted the plains to the foot of the hills. The fields glittered with gold and greens and ever-changing hues.

Now the only time I see the sunrise is if I happen to wake up early for a pee.

All the roads cutting through the Ochils are pretty much single track. Traffic is light and there are strategically placed passing places so you do get to where you want to go.

The road at the back of Dumyat runs down to Bridge of Allan. There is also a smaller road branching south that will take you down a single track road to Logie Kirk but beware, it has no passing places. It is a little used track because it is so steep and narrow. If you are unfortunate enough to meet someone coming up there is a good chance you might need to reverse as much as half a mile to find a suitable place to pass.

Logie Kirk and its Churchyard is a hidden gem. It nestles below Dumyat in a peaceful spot. I took Monkeydog for a walk around the Old Kirk and gravestones thinking I'd be ten minutes and I ended up spending over an hour. The oldest part of the of the cemetery is on the south side of the church. There are two Norse hogback stones (Viking sculptures believed to be grave markers) that hint at an earlier history but the earliest date inscribed (on a row of plain flat stones) is 1598.

I explored the cemetery with Monkeydog galloping in between the headstones. In the far corner, below the headstone of a ten-year old boy sat a simple stone. The poem engraved on it made me well up;

If Tears Could Build A
Stairway And Memories

A Lane. I'd Walk Right Up
To Heaven And Bring
You Home Again.

I made my way back down to the car park next to the new section of Logie Cemetery. A footpath, which passes the pleasant Witches Craig Caravan Park and stretches all the way to Tillicoultry, separates the two. It is well kept. I had a wander inside to the circular wall that houses a wooden bench to see what was on the marble plinth. It was another poem and just delightful;

Snowdrops
The World May Never Notice
If A Snowdrop Doesn't Bloom
Or Even Pauses To Wonder
If The Petals Fall Too Soon

But Every Life That Ever Forms
Or Ever Comes To Be
Touches The World In Some Small Way
For All Eternity

The Little One We Longed For
Was Swiftly Here And Gone
But The Love That Was Then Planted
Is A Light That Still Shines On

And Though Our Arms Are Empty
Our Hearts Know What To Do
Every Beating Of Our Hearts
Says That 'We Love You'

There were a dozen cars in the car park but I could only see one other person in the graveyard. A man in a blue anorak stood over a grave decorated with colourful carnations, tulips and gladioli. Head bowed, lost in thought and prayer. As loyal as Greyfriars Bobby. I imagine the owners of the other cars were adventurers. Bike racks adorned several of the cars.

Going uphill from Logie Kirk is an interesting challenge on a bicycle, even for top cyclists. Can you make it up without getting off and pushing? Unless you have been training for the *Tour De France*, don't even bother trying.

It is also an interesting challenge in a car. About a quarter of a mile into the ascent there is a hairpin bend that rises steeply making it a difficult manoeuvre. During a driving lesson for number one son I made him stop on the curve and forced him to do a hill start. It was thrilling, scary and all the more impressive that he made it. I had it in mind I might do the same with numbers two and three sons when they were learning - but I didn't want the expense of another new clutch. *#learnedmylesson.*

The easiest way to get to the Sheriffmuir Inn is from the Dunblane side. A signpost at the roundabout in the middle of the town will direct you up the hill. It's at the roundabout that gives you access to the town centre, the golf club and an Indian restaurant called India Gate, (which I can thoroughly recommend).

Travelling up the Sheriffmuir road from Dunblane you will get a glimpse of where the money is. First of all the road is bordered by drystane dykes. To the right, neat little white houses with manicured lawns. To the left, hedges obscure the larger gardens and even larger houses. Gardens on which you could build whole housing schemes. These are not gardens that require a little attention to now and again. These are gardens that require real work. Picture a young man chapping one of the doors and offering gardening services.

"Do you need a gardener?"

"Oh, yes, I need a dozen gardeners to keep this garden in check."

"How many gardeners have you got?"

"Twelve."

Further up the road takes a sharp turn north and there you will find a cluster of stone built houses - one of the police sergeants I worked with bought a cottage there. A nice place to bring up kids and in the winter, if it snows, they can always use a sledge to get to school. The road keeps climbing. Even further up newer houses are being built. Large timber clad affairs that would look even more magnificent if they weren't painted a ghastly shade of green.

Once the road plateaus, you will discover the site of The Battle of Sheriffmuir. There is a monument marking the spot where a Jacobite Army, composed of largely Highlanders under the command of the Earl of Mar met the Hanoverian Army consisting of mainly regular British soldiers under the Duke of Argyll. Both sides claimed victory. Historians will tell you the Earl of Mar led a parade rather than a war campaign. He had the advantage of larger numbers and could easily have seen off Argyll if he had had a little more fire in his belly.

I find it strange standing at the monument looking across the flattened moor. *Why would anyone pick that spot to do battle?* For a start the encounter was in November, it was bound to be cold and wet. *Why choose a boggy moor?*

It is like picking a fight at school and saying 'okay, I'll meet you later, across the river, through the other side of the forest, up a hill and round the back of the big rock. Most sensible people would say, 'Aye, nae bother,' light up their pipe, pour a beer and go and sit by the fire. I mean what are they going to do? Wait about a bit in the cold, then get upset? Come back around the rock, down the hill, through the forest, across the water and be angry you didn't show up? Well, yes, but they would also be cold and tired and more likely to go to bed.

War is mad, isn't it?

I often think about terrorists and other intemperate folks in the world and think maybe if you just took a drink and chilled out a bit. I mean look at President Trump, he doesn't drink. Someone take his Twitter off him and give him a dram, for goodness sake!.

The Earl of Mar and the Duke of Argyll might have been best friends if they had shared a bottle of malt. Even if they still felt a bit tetchy towards each other then put them in a boxing ring and let them sort out their differences. They don't have to bring their armies into it, do they?

So what was it all about?

Although the Kingdoms of Scotland and England had been united since 1707, not all Scots were happy with the marriage (even today it's about fifty/fifty). In particular, the Jacobites, supporters of the House of Stuart, sought to exploit the general unrest within Scottish society. In 1714 George the first was proclaimed King of Great Britain and Ireland, John Erskine, Earl of Mar, began to raise a Jacobite army in an attempt to return James Francis Edward Stuart, the Old Pretender, to the throne. In response, a combined government force of Scottish and English regiments commanded by the Duke of Argyll was dispatched to confront the rebels.

The two armies finally met each other on 13th November 1715 at Sheriffmuir. Although the Highland forces of the Jacobites greatly outnumbered those of the government (12,000 Jacobites to only 6,000 government soldiers), Mar was not an experienced military leader. In contrast, the government army comprised well trained regular troops led by a seasoned commander.

In the inconclusive battle that followed, both sides left the field claiming victory. The Earl of Mar, however, was forced to retreat with his demoralised force.

Moving on, literally, across the moor on a fairly well maintained piece of tarmac I arrive at The Sheriffmuir Inn. It was closed. There was a small sign in the window.

We apologise for any inconvenience however, the Sheriffmuir Inn has closed temporarily, we are refurbishing and have a planned opening date of Easter.

I was there at the end of June. There was no sign of any work going on and I was saddened to think this place might never be opened again to provide sustenance to a weary cyclist or coffee and cake to the odd tourist of an afternoon. At one time it served hearty dinners, pie and pints and even went gourmet serving delicious evening meals. Newspapers littered tables allowing interesting things to be discussed between long married couples. Each taking a different part of the paper and pointing out unusual, strange or shocking events.

"Rangers beat Celtic 3 - 2," he might say.

"Mary Berry is leaving *Bake Off*," she would reply.

The earthquake in Mexico, the threat of nuclear war and tensions in the middle-east passing over their collective interest.

I have fond memories of cycling to the Sheriffmuir Inn, underage drinking and hoping to catch a glimpse of the bear. Yes it was home to a bear.

Scottish Ladies Show-Jumping Champion Maggie Nimmo married British Commonwealth Wrestling Champion Andy Robin, and knew her family would be unusual, for with Andy came a nine-month old Hercules, a real live grizzly bear. Andy rescued Hercules from a wildlife park when it was just a cub. The wildlife park had nowhere to keep him and planned to put him down. Andy had the idea to make Hercules famous. Initially he planned to train Hercules to wrestle. Bear-handed, I suppose.

Hercules grew to 70 stone, 9ft tall and became a global superstar. He went on to star alongside Roger Moore in the James Bond film Octopussy, featured on the cover of Time Magazine, met Margaret Thatcher and even caddied for Bob Hope at Gleneagles. How brilliant is that? I can imagine Hercules asking Bob which club he wanted and Bob replying, "Surprise me".

Hercules had the run of their house and a fenced off area at the back of the Sheriffmuir Inn. It wasn't always I caught a glimpse of him but I could hear him grunting and moving around. That was when he was there, for Hercules travelled the world doing adverts, starring in films and making appearances.

When filming an advert in Benbecula in the Western Isles in August 1980, Hercules went walkabout. The landscape too much of an attraction for his bear genes.

Hercules was missing for twenty-four days. Local crofters eventually spotted him swimming across the tidal sands. A helicopter was mobilised and a vet managed to shoot him with a tranquilliser dart. More than three weeks in the unforgiving terrain of the Outer Hebrides took its toll on big Herc. Lack of food had made him abnormally thin. Andy and Maggie had to nurse him back to health. Owning a pub helped, probably, because Hercules had a liking for beer.

Hercules died on 4th February 2001, aged twenty-five. By that time Andy and Maggie had moved to a spread near Dollar they called their 'Big Bear Ranch.' Hercules was buried in the garden but when Andy and Maggie later decided to move, they reburied their beloved bear beneath the life-size statue of him erected in North Uist, a Mecca for his fans.

Andy had dyslexia, so Maggie Robin wrote a book about their time with Hercules. It is full of affection, sad in places but amusing too.

I hope someone opens the Sheriffmuir Inn again. It is such a beautiful spot.

Chapter eight

WICKED THINGS I SUSPECT

Press the pedal to the metal and zoom up the A9 towards Inverness from Perth and you will be on the most dangerous road in Scotland. Despite the surrounding beauty, it can be a frustrating drive stuck behind a lorry or a caravan. There are sections of dual carriageway that allow a blast of speed but overtaking seven or eight slow moving camper vans and four juggernauts only brings you up behind the next conga line of traffic. Perhaps it is the distractions on offer that make it such a perilous journey. As the drive takes you through the middle of the Grampian Mountains it is easy to take your eyes off the road to admire the majestic scenery. Thus I recommend you stop now and again to give yourself time to fill your eyes with the splendour and recharge your soul.

A mere twelve miles north of Perth, on opposite banks of the Tay, are the charming towns of Dunkeld and Birnam. Big tree country. I took the first exit, just before the train station, and drove through the village of Birnam. I could smell pine. A leafy tree lined road welcomed me into the small village before coming across quiet cottages where I imagine many depraved things go on. Scissor cut lawns, squared away hedges and immaculate facades show the occupants like to keep themselves busy. Spending hours in their gardens manicuring lawns, weeding borders and clipping bushes. So what happens when the sun disappears or the heavens open and rain pours down for three days at a time? What do all those inhabitants turn their attention to, I ask you?

Wicked things I suspect.

I may not be the only one to feel the brooding malevolence behind every door. Shakespeare received his inspiration for his 'Scottish play' in this area. Take a trip to the 'Birnam Oak' and you might see why. The tree is found in a strip of woodland on the south bank of the River Tay. I parked up and walked down a narrow lane towards the river and came out at a well-worn footpath where a signpost directed me west. A few yards on I saw a tall gnarled looking tree and thought that must be it. What looked like a gravestone was embedded in the ground beside it. The stone was engraved with the words, *'It's not me - I'm a sycamore...'* I laughed. The next tree on the path had a similar gravestone that said, *'Not me either - Keep going...'* Amusing me no end.

I reached the Birnam Oak. The gnarled old tree stretched out like octopus tentacles, some branches impossibly low, like gangling limbs ready to grab unsuspecting passers-by. It is easy to imagine a trio of witches underneath, stirring at their cauldron as they cackled and crowed. Shakespeare's *Macbeth* sat spellbound by the crones, listening to their prophecy that one day he would be King of Scotland. A foretelling under this thousand year old tree that consumed him with sufficient desire to murder King Duncan. But then the deed wracked him with so much guilt it became his curse. Therein lies tragedy of Macbeth.

A shiver went through my spine and fleeting thoughts of the macabre, probably more to do with the chill wind caressing the back of my neck. Birnam is actually a nice place. It is dark and foreboding in the forest but, with a stout pair of boots and a waterproof, it is a fine place to walk a dog. If that is not to your taste, there is always the *Beatrix*

Potter Exhibition & Garden where you can immerse the family in the world of a Victorian classroom.

Back in the car I passed the *Birnam Village Shop*, it is the 'best-one' according to the sign above the entrance door. A fact I couldn't argue with because I saw no other shop, so no competition. A little further on is the grandiose *Birnham Hotel*. Large railings, the likes you would see at Buckingham Palace, hinted at the delights of the gardens attached to it but I continued on. The turn off to Dunkeld took me over the River Tay, across a bridge built by Thomas Telford.

I like driving over rivers into towns, they make clear boundary lines. A short crossing over a bridge and you are there. Large cities tend to merge into the countryside, speed limits slow the pace to a dawdle. Mile after mile of nothing but the sprawl of houses lived in by those who want the excitement of the city but end up spending half their lives waiting for a gap in the traffic.

Dunkeld doesn't have that problem, its boundary is confined by the river on one side and the steep hill on the other. It has developed a quaintness that is both charming and mysterious. On my first visit I drove through the busy main street. Cars vied to find a parking spot on either side of the road and that made it a slow traverse which is fine. People gave way to others with patience. There is no-one rushing to get anywhere. The side streets promise something of interest. I wondered what delights I might come across.

I like Dunkeld, there are no depravities to speak of, unlike its neighbour. My first visit there was to the golf course to deliver numbers two and three sons, who were playing in a junior county match. At the far side of the village a signpost directed us uphill to the course, a climb that strained the car. The road to the car park splits the 8th and 18th holes. Walking the course requires several steep climbs and subsequent descents. It is an interesting course, but tiring. Golfers do well to play to their handicap because there are often difficult conditions. Changing weather and blustering winds test the faint hearted.

My last visit to Dunkeld was to celebrate the day my mother became an octogenarian. Our extended family booked General Wade's House in the grounds of *The Dunkeld Hotel* which nestles in an idyllic spot by the River Tay found at the far side of Dunkeld and along a mile long driveway. Our family travelled en masse and arrived early enough to park up and explore the delights of Dunkeld before settling into our accommodation.

The town of Dunkeld promises interesting nooks and crannies to explore, it didn't disappoint. *The Taybank* pub has benches outside where couples sip beer and wine. A sign advertised the evening entertainment as a 'Friend's Fiddle Night'. Shops are named after their owners. This makes them much more inviting than the chain store variety you get in every other town and city. Seen one, seen them all. There is little of that tat and glare in Dunkeld, you never know what you will find in the shops here.

A store selling climbing gear and outdoorsy things also advertised massages. You don't get that in *Sportsdirect or even Marks & Spencers,* do you?

'Ella's of Dunkeld' despite being a small shop has enough clothes to keep Mrs McEwan interested for an hour which furrowed my brow because they were expensive enough to require an additional top up on the credit card.

The Co-op store is the only non-independent in the row of shops.

The High Street is off the main through road and has a narrow cobbled entrance but opens out like a pair of scissors. Curio shops on either side squirrel away many treasures. I spent a pleasant hour wandering from one to the other. Outside I admired the ornate fountain that sits in the middle of the road and acts as a roundabout. Cars can circle around it and drive back up out of the High Street.

Tucked away in the corner is an old stone building. Artworks adorn the entrance hall and the wall leading upstairs to the Dunkeld Art Exhibition. It has an impressive range of work from more than one hundred artists. I set Mrs McEwan the challenge to find her favourite picture. I looked for my own favourite and settled on a vibrant blue street scene of a *Summer Evening in Pitlochry* by Colm O'Brien. Mrs McEwan opted for a pencil drawing of an expressive dog called *Snow Springer* by Rosie Johnson, I think that was my second favourite.

I always try to choose a favourite picture at an art gallery or my favourite exhibit at a museum when I visit these places. It gives a purpose to the visit. It makes me look with an appreciative and critical eye. What works? What interests me? What would I put up in my home? I pay more attention. I become absorbed in the process and I get more out of it. It helps me remember the visit too. It is such a nice thing to be able to take someone back to a gallery and say, 'Let me show you my favourite painting.'

In the other corner of the High Street is a narrow lane of whitewashed cottages leading to the impressive Dunkeld Cathedral. I couldn't help thinking that in days gone by Dunkeld must have held a strategic position guarding passage from the Lowlands to the Highlands of Scotland. It is somewhat unexpected for this little sleepy backwater today to have such an imposing structure.

Dunkeld Cathedral is a venerable ruin set amid beautiful shaded lawns which overlook the River Tay. It has been repaired at various stages throughout the centuries and is now in the hands of Historic Scotland. The choir was re-roofed in 1908 courtesy of Sir Donald Currie, a generous benefactor who had made his fortune in shipping. The choir is still used today as a place of worship. Entry is free and they lay on little handheld electronic devices that play an interesting account of the history of the building.

A room at the rear of the pulpit holds the tomb of Alexander Stewart, 'The Wolf of Baddenoch,' who *The Scotsman* newspaper described as Scotland's vilest man. Stewart, also known as the 'Celtic Attila,' had an appetite for death and destruction that was simply petrifying. A beastly beast, even by 14th century Scotland standards.

Alexander Stewart was gifted land from his father that stretched from Moray to the Pentland Firth. He abused his power by maintaining a systematic rule of terror across much of the Highlands, imprisoning and murdering those who offended him. He pillaged the countryside and set fire to entire villages. Stewart added to his landholdings by marrying Eupheme de Ross, Countess of Ross. They had no children which he blamed on his wife as Stewart fathered around forty illegitimate children with other women.

The church, on hearing of his violent ways, censured him and sent a monk to his residence at Lochindorb Castle to inform him of his excommunication. Lochindorb Castle sits on a partly man-made island in a remote loch on the bleak Dava Moor south of Nairn. Like many Scottish Castles,

Lochindorb had a deeply unpleasant dungeon accessible only by a trap door in the ceiling of the subterranean prison. Because of its island location it had three feet of water covering the floor, and this is where the Wolf of Bannedoch consigned the messenger monk.

One bath he could have done without.

The excommunication sparked a spree of violence. The Wolf of Baddenoch and a bunch of his fellow wild and wicked men plundered the town of Forres. They then destroyed Pluscarben Abbey en route to Elgin. There they burned much of the town and destroyed Elgin Cathedral, the second largest cathedral in Scotland. Such fit of pique not seen again until my number three son wasn't allowed an ice-cream as punishment for not eating his veg.

The Wolf of Baddenoch's older brother, Robert III, who had only just succeeded to the throne, gave him a rap on the knuckles. Robert called upon the Wolf of Baddenoch to do penance for his crimes and pay significant reparations: then, as family do, he pardoned him.

Legend has it that during a violent storm in 1394 a man dressed in black visited the Wolf of Baddenoch and challenged him to a game of chess. In the morning the mysterious visitor had gone. The servants were found dead outside the castle walls, killed by lightning. The Wolf of Baddenoch was found dead in the banqueting hall, his boots had been ripped from his feet with such force it had torn out the nails. The man who had wrought so much fear on those within his lands had himself been terrorised to death. Such are the perils of playing chess with the devil.

Our plan was to have lunch with Gran and Papa and my boys. I scouted out and booked *Howies Bistro* for lunch. It is on the main road. We were late, having stopped to explore *'Kettles of Dunkeld'* a knick-knack shop that is like the Tardis and had me drooling to buy things I would never use. Perhaps I am getting older and wiser? I only bought one thing, a salad spinner. It ended up in a cupboard beside a similar one I'd purchased ten years ago and forgot about.

Howies did not let us down. The food was delicious and abundant. Soup and crusty bread doesn't get much better than this. I had the chicken, chorizo and balsamic syrup panini. My boys ordered various burgers and was goggle-eyed when I saw the size of the portions. My boys might not be able for their four course dinner at night. The eyes of the octogenarian sitting next to me bulged bigger than her belly and the only thing she complained about was she wouldn't be able to eat another thing all day. *She did though. I don't know how she does it.* One last comment about *Howies Bistro*, the staff were great, pleasant cheery people who couldn't do enough for us. If you own a bistro, café or restaurant and want your place to be the best it can be, take your staff there first to see how to do it properly.

We left *Howies Bistro* and emerged back onto the street loosening belts and waddling in happiness. Before lunch we were all keen to head back to the leisure pool at the Hilton and have a swim. We weren't so keen now. Instead we crossed the road and explored *The Vintage Shop*, had a look in the window at the country bakery to admire the cakes, noted the flat above *The Craft Cupboard* was no longer up for sale and we popped into *The Atholl Gallery* to admire the eclectic mix of objet d'art.

The next day we had lunch at *'The Meeting Place'* a bar within the *Atholl Arms Hotel*. It sold interesting beers, which were to my taste. The food loosened a smile when it arrived and we had to loosen our belts afterwards.

Dunkeld isn't a big town but I like it. I like that it is unusual. I like that it is quaint and I like that for such a small place I could happily spend an afternoon wandering its shops and an evening drinking in its pubs, with the distinct possibility of being entertained by a gregarious local. I am not the only one to like it. It is popular with visitors from all over the world. I hope it doesn't change in character to accommodate its growing tourist trade. Places like Dunkeld maintain their charm by steering away from the norm.

Chapter nine

SLIPPERS, PUPPY HUGS, AND A WEE DRAM

This wasn't any old excuse to get away.

Mrs McEwan and I headed north to spend the weekend with her old school friend, Aileen, on holiday with her hubby from Australia. We met Aileen and Marty for lunch in Grantown-on-Spey outside a four and a half star *TripAdvisor* rated coffee shop. As soon as the old schoolgirl chums saw each other they emitted a high-pitched shriek, grabbed each other and bounced up and down on the pavement, boobs and hair flying in all directions.

When grown women haven't seen each other for a while why do they squeal like new-born piglets? The longer the time apart the louder the squealing. Is it like a build-up of gases in the stomach looking for a release? I don't know, but here was Mrs McEwan and her old friend, grabbing each other like they were drowning and giving a good imitation of punk rockers at a *Sex Pistols* concert. Their glee might easily have been misinterpreted as conjoined twins walking on hot coals, such was their unintelligible screech. I think they both let out a little wee.

Marty and I shook hands and edged away from the women, distancing ourselves from the scene they were making, hoping the incoherent babble wouldn't go on for the full twenty minutes like the last time they met. It didn't. After nineteen minutes and thirty seconds they calmed down and we persuaded them to enter the coffee shop. Before we even sat down the two of them disappeared off to the toilet, further evidence they had weed themselves.

High St. Merchant's Café served fine cappuccino and cake. With the aroma of roasted coffee, comfy chairs and fresh sesame seed bagels it is a place to calm the soul. Ideal for catching up with friends or admiring the gallery. Hard not to be happy here, yet an elderly couple at the next table ate their lunch in complete silence. Down-turned mouths made them look like sad clowns without makeup.

He wore a flat tweed cap and her pink rinse was held in place by a blue bandana. They say couples grow to look alike and in this case it was true. They wore their wrinkled faces like crumpled newspaper. The only time they opened their mouths was when they picked up small samples of their food on their forks, one bite at a time, and took it on board to chew the life out of it. They glanced at each other with utter contempt and no doubt wondered which of the two of them would die first. I got the distinct impression neither of them cared who went first.

After lunch, and following the obligatory purchases of memorabilia in a craft shop called 'ewe & me,' we left Grantown to travel in convoy to Dufftown. Marty and I glad of the respite. Peace from listening to our wives gibbering away as only old female friends do.

It is a nice drive from Grantown-on-Spey to Dufftown, a distance just short of thirty miles. The A95 follows the south side of the River Spey, the fastest flowing river in Scotland. The Spey is as important for its salmon fishing as it is for whisky production. Rising in the Central Highlands, at over one hundred miles long, it supports many local industries before spilling into the Moray Firth five miles west of Buckie. As we left Grantown the road took us to a stone bridge crossing the river. The waters looked black and menacing, not dirty like the Thames, just opaque and ominous. During the drive it disappeared behind rows of fat green pine trees but when it caught our sight the waters sped along crashing into random boulders, declaring its resolve to make it to the sea.

I wanted to have a look at something of interest before getting to Dufftown so I continued on the A941 past our turnoff and by-passing Craigellachie. In a quarter of a mile we crossed the River Spey again on a functional and ordinary bridge, designed to take modern cars in as straight a line as the countryside allows. Upstream there is another crossing, the original Craigellachie Bridge. A proper crossing. Built by Thomas Telford in 1814 it is a single arch cast iron construction, the oldest cast iron bridge in Scotland and, oh boy, is it beautiful. Standing fifteen feet high on each side of the river, it features two sets of mock-medieval turrets with arrow slits and crenellated battlements. It is now only a foot crossing. We turned around and took the side road off down to the bridge where we parked up and walked down to the river. The Craigellachie Bridge is even more impressive from the water's edge. The single span extends one-hundred and fifty feet across the Spey, a revolutionary design for its time.

Thomas Telford created quite the legacy. He was a prolific designer of projects for Scotland's infrastructure. He was nicknamed the 'Colossus of Roads', which is clever don't you think?

Marty and I tried skimming stones, an obligatory pastime for males. Anytime we are in the vicinity of water we look for ammunition. It didn't last long, there being an insufficient supply of aerodynamic pebbles, so we headed on to Dufftown and our respective B&Bs.

Dufftown is in the heart of Speyside and whisky country. Within a twelve-mile radius you will find the distilleries of *Glen Grant, Cardhu, Knockando, Tamdhu, The Macallan Estate, Balvenie, Glendullan, Dailuaine, Aberlour, Glenfiddich, Mortlach, Kininvie, Allt-a-Bhainne, Strathmill, Glenfarclas* and, as you would expect, the *Dufftown Distillery*. It is entirely possible I missed one. If you like whisky trails and tours then Dufftown is the ideal base to kill off those parts of your liver not yet succumbed to cirrhosis.

Our B&B was at the east side of Dufftown, a place called *Dullan Brae*. A big old house with not much room from the pavement to the front door but large grounds to one side and the rear. Not a place to own if you don't like gardening. As we were soon to realise, not a place to own of you don't like renovating either.

The delightful couple who own Dullan Brae work hard to make it one of the best B&Bs I have ever visited. Theresa met us at the door and politely asked us to remove our shoes in the porch. Unusual for a B&B but once we entered and saw the lush cream carpets and the pride she took in her house, it was understandable. She issued us with complimentary slippers, which was a nice touch.

As Theresa showed us to our room she chatted enthusiastically about Dullan Brae and the huge renovations they had undertaken. I had been against staying there because our room wasn't en-suite. I like to get up in the morning go for a pee without having to bother about getting dressed first, other guests might not approve of a hairy fifty-something wandering about in his pants. As it turned out, we were the only guests on the top floor and had the bathroom all to ourselves. Theresa allocated us the 'blue room,' the best room in the house. It is massive. It has a separate dressing room which is bigger than our bedroom at home. A big bay window gave us views over the Mortlach Brewery. Dullan Brae had once been owned by the founder of the distillery.

Hanging in the dressing room were the cosiest luxury dressing gowns you can imagine. Just scrummy, honestly, they were like wearing puppy hugs. There would be no trip to the loo wearing just pants with those around.

We dumped our bags and Theresa gave us a tour of the rest of the B&B. We had access to a large sitting room with comfy leather sofas and a kitchen stocked with nuts, chocolate and several malt whiskies (first dram free). I would have been happy to curl up on the couch and read a book, but we had arranged to meet up with Aileen and Marty.

Aileen had booked a tour of the Glenfiddich Distillery. The distillery is only half-a-mile walk. We had plenty time, so we sauntered up the main street. Dufftown is clean and very pretty. We admired the clock tower at the crossroads, which displayed the correct time on all four sides. The tower is built from grey and pink granite, it has mock circular gun loops and overhanging dummy turrets on each of its four sides and is known as 'the clock that hanged MacPherson.'

The story goes that MacPherson, a local lad, was convicted and condemned to death for some trumped up crime. An appeal to the King had successfully brought him a pardon but the sheriff, Lord Braco, put the clock forward fifteen minutes to ensure MacPherson would hang before the pardon arrived. What a dastardly trick to play on anyone.

Opposite the clock tower is the marvellous *Dufftown Whisky Shop*. An absolute Alladin's cave of whiskies, you name it they supplied it. To the delight of the girls they were having a gin tasting day. Marty and I immersed ourselves in examining the hundreds of choices of malts on offer and our wives giggled away, ever louder, as they sampled each of the seven taster gins on offer. Mike, the proprietor, knew his stuff and Vicky, who had a cheery way about her, made the visit even more pleasant. We put several bottles aside for collection later, what great service.

We left the shop with a rosy glow in our cheeks and walked down to the distillery. The Glenfiddich Distillery is in a lovely setting. Low stone walls and manicured lawns guide you into the visitor centre. A pub with outside tables, surrounded by tubs full of colourful flowers looked inviting, but we had our appointment. Aileen had booked the 3 p.m. tour, and we just had enough time to pop to the toilet before it started. The tour guide called out the names of the visitors on her list. Each made their way through to the ante-chamber until the four of us were left standing on our own. Our names appeared to be missing from the list. Aileen confronted the receptionist, who looked for our names on her computer.

"I don't see your name on the list, when did you book it?"

"About three months ago. I booked it from Australia."

"We don't seem to have your name. Our 3 p.m. tour is now full up, I'm afraid."

Not put off, Aileen, produced her smart phone from her pocket. "Well it just so happens I have a copy of the booking right here on my phone."

This is what Aileen revels in. She is a smart cookie; you don't get to be a doctor without dogged determination. She doesn't suffer fools, I've seen her rapier tongue cut the legs off jobsworths before. Aileen was more than a little peeved they had lost her booking. She was here to enjoy herself with old friends and wasn't about to have that scuppered. With the receptionist adamant the tour was full and Aileen single-mindedly thumbing her way through her smart phone for her confirmation email I gathered things might get a little crotchety.

"There it is!" she announced triumphant and promptly wedged it in front of the receptionists face.

The receptionist calmly looked at the email.

"Yes, this booking is for today, and you have the correct time 3 p.m. and it is indeed for four people," she smiled at Aileen, "but this booking is for The Macallan Estate Distillery, this is the Glenfiddich Distillery."

"Well, I'll be the daughter of a dingo," Aileen said throwing her arms up in the air in defeat.

We all burst out laughing.

The Macallan Estate, is only ten minutes away, if you have a helicopter - we didn't. So we booked the 4 p.m. Glenfiddich tour and popped into the bar to kill an hour. The bar, I have to say, is excellent. It had a great choice of whiskies, as you would expect, but also nice beer, various ciders and a generous selection of gins. We ordered and took our drinks up a spiral staircase to a comfortable spot in front of the fireplace. It was ideal. I thoroughly recommend an hour of drinking before a distillery tour. I can recommend the Glenfiddich tour too. Our guide, a cheery, ginger-haired woman, couldn't have been more informative. She enthused over the Glenfiddich whisky and later, at the tasting, she enjoyed a sample as much as the next man.

The walk back into Dufftown took a little longer than the walk there. Two young photogenic Highland Cows in a field saw to that. Our interest in them matched by their interest in us. Google Cloud now hosts a few hundred additional photos of the hairy beasts.

We had booked the Tannochbrae Restaurant in Fife Street for dinner. Rather than heading back to our respective B&Bs, as was the initial plan, we stopped in at *The Royal Oak* for an apéritif. The Royal Oak, sold a good range of real ales, not a big place but quirky. It was busy, but still easy to spot the locals, who were all drinking *Tennents Lager*.

An odd bunch of leather-clad males stood to attention at the bar. A game of football was playing on the small television screen in the corner and with that mutual interest I got talking to them. They were from Norway. They told me every year they bike all the way across Europe to make their way to Dufftown to sample our whiskies. Six motorcyclists on the whisky trail. One of them raised his arm to attract the barmaid's attention. His hand just stopped short of being a Nazi salute. I wondered if I was in fact talking with a group of Norwegian bikers. They could all have been members of the modern equivalent of the Gestapo for all I knew. Everyone of them looked like a serial killer. I returned to my companions and kept one eye on the serial killer convention until they left. I imagine, being trained in the dark arts, they spotted my impromptu surveillance and made a tactical retreat.

We remained there chatting until it was time to navigate the thirty yards to the restaurant. The Royal Oak, has since been refurbished and changed its name to *The Seven Stills.* It no longer sells ale on draught, which seems a shame for all the CAMRA fans. It is now more a restaurant than a pub and I note it is getting a reputation for great cooking.

We were hungry. It was time to eat.

Tannochbrae is a guest house and restaurant, maintained in pristine condition. Outside the woodwork looks crisp and fresh. The small multi-paned front door, brilliant white with a green surround. Hanging baskets and half-barrel flower pots straddle the door, splashing the place with colour. Two flags sit halfway up the wall and salute those entering. Despite the menu and awards on open display, it is not the type of restaurant I normally visit. I like big open inviting doors. This is a converted house and once you are over the threshold in these places, it is hard to turn around and walk out again without giving offence. Liquored up and ravenous enough not to bother about that we barged on in.

Ben greeted us in the foyer, the face of a young man in his teens but he was tall, wide and muscular. Like Arnold Schwarzenegger in his younger days. We christened him Big Ben. Unlike his London counterpart, Big Ben had a much softer side to him. His film-star looks and charming manner caught the eye of the ladies. He took our coats and showed us through to the conservatory for a pre-dinner drink. We passed through a small but delightful bar, jam packed with whiskies. The conservatory had leather bound chairs, to sink into. It was all so comfortable; we grinned like lemon-sharks at our good fortune. But the real treat was still to come.

Our table ready, Big Ben escorted us to the restaurant. All six of the serial killer convention we had seen in the pub were sat at the adjacent table. I did a double take. They had changed out of their leathers and no longer looked like a group of modern day Gestapo on tour. They were quite friendly. We engaged in teasing banter and I commended them on their ability to consume copious amounts of whisky, with no outward effect on their bearing. With their affable approach they lulled me into thinking I might be wrong about them. Maybe they were what they said they were, a group of middle-aged Norwegians indulging in their passion for motorcycle travel, whisky and Scotland. That was until Big Ben informed us the scallops were off the menu.

"What! Who ate all the scallops?" I said, squinting at the Norwegians.

"Har de har. Vee hav eaten all zee scallops," they taunted.

I went back to thinking I was right. They were latter-day serial killers on convention, right enough.

Our attention turned to the menu.

We each chose a different starter, and they were all scrumptious. My Craigellachie Smoked Salmon and Black Pudding salad was exquisite. Then the mains arrived. My ordinary rump steak was anything but ordinary, the cow whose rump had provided this offering was a special cow. A cow revered as the god of all Scottish cows. I could hardly contain my delight, but a few seconds later my joy was cruelly dashed.

Mrs McEwan's food arrived, Glenrinnes Pheasant Breast with black forest ham and red currant sauce, passed to her right under my nose. The heady aroma was all too much, it smelled wonderful and despite my perfect steak, I now wanted that. I waited until Mrs McEwan popped to the loo and took a forkful – it was glorious.

Our mains came with a crunchy medley of veg. My companions raved about the carrots done in a butter and honey sauce but the piping hot, cheesy cauliflower and broccoli was my favourite. God's nourishment in heaven. I sneaked the last bit by directing my companions' attention to the decorative antler lampshade.

A similar thing happened with the sweet. My crumble was tart and lovely, but the sticky toffee pudding, ordered by Mrs McEwan, came with a whisky flavoured ice cream so alluring I grabbed my spoon and stole a chunk. Oh how I wish I'd ordered that too.

Sated, we ordered coffee and chatted with the other guests. I formulated a plan to oust the serial killers using a trick I learned in the police. There are many methods you can use to catch a liar, like testing their knowledge backwards. Get them to run through their story in reverse. The last thing they did first, all the way back to the start. Liars rarely maintain an accurate chronological account when they tell their story backwards. Be courteous, don't interrogate, it's all in the detail. I asked the first three where they had been, what sights they had seen and what whiskies they had tried. Then I asked the last three where they had visited last, what sight they saw before the last one and which whisky they tried before last.

They passed. I was dealing with professionals.

My next tact was to check their knowledge, again it's all in the detail. If they were Norwegian, then they would be able to answer questions about Norway. All I had to do was catch them out. I searched my brain for information I had stored about the country; *Is the capital Oslo? Or is that Finland? They have fjords, but everyone knows that.*

I needed something only a Norwegian would know. And then I remembered a radio show I'd listened to. Norway has a phone number anyone from around the world can dial that allows them to speak to a random Norwegian. The idea is people can call up and talk to one of their citizens - a person who has signed up to be a de facto ambassador - they receive no training whatsoever and no instructions about what to say (or more to the point what not to say). A tourist gimmick perhaps. The radio show I'd listened to called the number and spoke to a young man, who politely answered all questions. I bet every Norwegian would know about the number, but a Gestapo serial killer might not.

"Did any of you sign up as ambassadors for the random number thing?"

"Sorry ze what?"

"The random number thingy that your country does."

They looked at each other blank. I was onto something. If all six hadn't heard of it then I was on the way to proving my theory.

"Ah! Wait, do you mean ze Swedish number?"

"Swedish number?"

"Yes, zis vas something ze Swedish did last year. Zay hav to close that program."

"They closed it?" I queried.

"Yes, too many provocative calls. Ze only thing people wanted to know was about the Swedes was the colour of zeir underwear," and all six Gestapo scallop thieves howled with laughter.

Big Ben's Dad (owner and chef) came out and talked to us afterwards. A nice touch. He looked so young he could have been Ben's older brother. We had heard a lot of good things about him from the locals, and they were right. He received our praise for his food with a humble pride.

I'm being serious now. The food at Tannochbrae is so tasty I want no one else to go there. I want to be able to book a table anytime I am back within a hundred miles of the place. It served the best food I have eaten anywhere in the world - and I've been to Burger King, KFC and Nandos.

Weighted down with three splendid courses of Scottish fare and a sense of harmony, we bade farewell to our hosts. I shook hands with each member of the serial killer convention thinking I'm so satisfied with life they could kill me now. Big Ben got cuddles from the wives that lasted a little too long for his comfort. And off we strolled on a balmy evening in Dufftown back to our respective B&Bs.

Whenever I get the chance to talk to Americans, I like to test their knowledge. I ask simple questions: What is the capital of France? Name the four countries which make up the UK? Why on earth did you vote for Donald Trump? That kind of thing. Their answers never fail to make me gasp and often it explains how Trump ended up as president. In fairness, Americans might like to test our knowledge too: How many states are there in America? What is the state capital of Wisconsin? Why on earth did you make Boris Johnson Foreign Secretary?

So when we arrived back at Dullan Brae and found three young adult Australians in the guest sitting room we settled in beside them. Whisky nightcaps in hand I got around to testing their knowledge too. Their awareness of the world, I have to say, was impressive. With hardly a question wrong we snuggled in for a good blether and another wee dram.

A wee dram. The spirit of Scotland. Pour the amber liquid neat, on ice or with a drop of water. Sipped and swirled around the mouth or glugged, however you take it. Once swallowed it burns the throat and warms the belly. The mood lightens, cheeks glow and a feeling of camaraderie overcomes us. *Is there any better way to start a morning?*

You'll have a wee dram? Is not so much am invitation in Scotland as an instruction. Whisky is, of course, a cure all. No matter what ailment you present someone will suggest a wee dram to heal the ill. Something to kill the germs, ease the pain or bring life back to a severed limb. The oldest lady in the UK is Grace Catherine Jones, born in 1906 she is still going strong. She still has all her faculties and puts her longevity down to two things: She never worries about anything and a nightly dram of whisky. She has a little nip of whisky before bedtime. When asked what her doctor said about her habit she replied, "Well, I got to one hundred and he said maybe I should put a little drop of water in it."

We had quite a selection of whiskies to choose from. I brought down the various malts I had purchased as did the Australians, and we set each other a blind taste test. I had a sip of a peaty malt that reminded me of a snuffed candle. Another reminded me of a holiday in Butlins Ayr, I don't know why it brought back that memory but it did. The last one they had a hint of citrus and marzipan, it was delicious.

I can't profess to be a connoisseur of whisky. I don't have the nose for it. I'm not a super-taster. My tongue has insufficient taste buds to be in that category. I liked the last one though.

"What is that?"

My new Australian friends smiled like it was an in-joke, then handed me the bottle. This was a single malt scotch whisky, aged 12 years, but it was unbranded. I checked the label.

Distilled and bottled in Scotland for Co-operative Group LTD.

Gobsmacked, flabbergasted, staggered, and bowled-over, I reached into my bag and pulled out a branded malt, aged 15 years, that tasted identical. None of us could differentiate between the two. My bottle cost twice the price, yet they were impossible to tell apart, at least to us. I've now tried various unbranded malts from all the supermarkets and when I make the comparison to more expensive malts, there is always one that matches it for taste. The only difference is the price. Now if that isn't worth the cost of this book and a five star review - I don't know what is.

A wee note from Malky.

I hope you are enjoying it so far, finding it both informative and fun. Would you be so kind as to give it a rating on Amazon, please? One way to help establish this book's status as an entertaining and valued source for visitors to Scotland is for others to read your esteemed opinion and customer review of the book.

Many thanks.

Malky

Come morning, we required copious amounts of coffee. So we made sure we made it in time for breakfast. Even better than the puppy hug dressing gowns are the owners. Dreamy Derek took charge of grilling the toast. Gorgeous Theresa worked hard on getting our bacon and eggs just right. Together they are a smashing couple. When the time came, we were sad to leave. The Australians joined us in the hall, all kisses and cuddles, as we carted our bags out to the car.

Instead of taking the A9 back home I put the Jag into dynamic mode and traversed the Cairngorms. The B9008 took us to Tomintoul where we joined the A939 and headed south. It follows the Old Military Road built after the Jacobite rising of 1745. They built the Military Roads to allow rapid deployment of Government forces to key locations in the Highlands. More than 250 miles of these roads were built under the command of General Wade linking forts in the Great Glen between Fort William and Inverness.

Our journey cut through exposed landscapes with never-ending views over mountains, it is a remote and untamed land. I was smitten. My breath taken away around each corner and every crest.

The road layout suited the Jag with incredible curves, dips and climbs. Like being on a cushioned rollercoaster. The rise to the Ski Centre on the Lecht is glorious. Out of season the slopes are snow free and the centre just as bare, with not a single vehicle in the car park. Over the top of the Lecht the horizon lowered and the blue sky wrapped around it like a gigantic duvet. The hills looked as if they would go on forever as the road disappeared into a crevasse in the distance.

108

Dufftown to Braemar is fifty miles. It didn't feel like fifty miles. I was a teenager again infatuated with my first car but with police training and years of driving experience. The police driving course required us to recite a spiel when we got behind the wheel. It went through my head; *Today, as all days, I will drive this car according to the system of car control which is a system or drill each feature of which will be considered in sequence, by me the driver, at the approach to any hazard. To do this requires my utmost concentration which is the full application of mind and body towards a particular endeavour and my endeavour today is to drive the car safely, smoothly, progressively and well.*

My emphasis was on progressively.

Accelerating for half the distance I could see to be clear, looking for vanishing points, reaching the apex of a corner then using the three-litre engine to power me through. At any moment I expected to see a *Top Gear* helicopter filming their new presenter line-up of Clarkson, Hammond, May and McEwan. It would make good television. The road from Dufftown to Braemar is simply spectacular.

Braemar, despite being over a thousand feet above sea level, is surrounded by well-wooded, lofty hills, which effectively shelter it from winter winds. It is an attractive place. The first building we see is *Braemar Castle* with its castellated turrets and star shaped curtain wall, followed by the handsome *Invercauld Arms Hotel.* The traditional stone building heralds a formality to be observed, yet outside the wooden tables sprawled with smiling and animated tourists awaiting lunch in the sun. A full Scottish breakfast that morning was the only thing that prevented me from stopping.

Braemar hosts its 'Gathering' or Highland Games in September. For such a small village it attracts large crowds. It has run the Games in its present form since 1832, although there has been a 'Gathering' there since the days of King Malcolm Canmore, nine hundred years ago.

In the midst of fine scenery, and the best centre for excursions into the Eastern Grampians, Braemar is a popular resort. It is clean, and for a busy tourist village it does well to maintain such high standards. The climate is dry (when it is not raining), the air remarkably unpolluted and invigorating. It is easy to imagine the locals as strapping lads and lassies, given to wearing kilts, tossing cabers and marching home to the sound of bagpipes.

The area was also an inspiration to Robert Louis Stevenson for it was here he created *Treasure Island*, his first great work. He based many of the characters on the people living in Braemar at the time. Locations in the book are similar to those found around Upper Deeside - and subject matters such as buried treasure have their origins in Braemar folk legends and history. The 1881 census showed that John Silver was head of a family living in Braemar when Robert Louis Stevenson was there.

The A93 from Braemar to Blairgowrie continued to delight. Within nine miles we had risen to the Glenshee Ski Centre. From there the road descends on a 12% gradient. A warning sign advises a low gear and another of a slippery road. Treacherous in winter but today, with a great drop to a babbling burn below it was a thrill. The tumbling waters below sparkled in the sun and filled my core with pride. I can't imagine a more glorious setting.

In six miles we levelled off at Spittal of Glenshee having dropped over a thousand feet in altitude. We passed the *Dalmunzie Estate* and glimpsed the *Glenbeag Mountain Lodges* through the trees. Cottages and barns appeared with increasing frequency as the land tamed. The burn widened but at this lower level became harder to spot through the trees and bushes. It dawned on me the Jag was no longer sweeping along and I had, unwittingly, slowed to a pleasant chunter. I switched dynamic mode off and purred along until a sign welcomed me to Blairgowrie and Rattray, 'twinned with Fergus, Ontario and Pleasanton, California', it said. Which sounds more like quadruplets than twins.

I had a satisfied feeling in my belly, like I'd just finished another three course dinner at Tannochbrae. Replete with the abundance of thrills the drive provided. It felt like the scenery had given me another puppy hug.

That's what Scotland does to you.

Chapter ten

CASTLE GLOOM

In ancient times a travelling Scot by the name of Argyll came upon a wide pasture in a valley below the Ochil Hills. There a romantic stream bubbled down the glen feeding the ground with fresh, vibrant water. Smitten with the green and fertile land, Argyll drew his claymore and plunged it into the soil, staking his claim to the 'Doll-ar' (Gaelic for broad meadow).

Argyll settled there to farm the land. He tamed the wild pasture and others joined him. A settlement grew in the foothills that was to become the town of Dollar. Argyll took a wife, and she bore him children. Life took on a new meaning.

But these were turbulent times, others arrived who coveted the land. This weighed heavy on Argyll's shoulders, he now had a family to protect. So he set about protecting his kin. Stone by stone, he built a stronghold in the narrow gorges of the glen. Each rock carried from miles around, heaved with blood, sweat and tears up the steep slope. He chose a rocky promontory to build his castle. With robust foundations his fortress rose into the sky, commanding a view over the village below. Imposing and powerful. With a chasm to the front, ravines to either side and a thick wall stretching up to the heavens it became invincible. A sturdy bastion capable of repelling all aggressors. It has remained impregnable to this day - unless you have the £6 entrance fee.

Originally called Castle Gloom, the Clan Campbell acquired it in the 15th-century and it became Castle Campbell. It is one of the most dramatically positioned castles in Scotland

and has one of the best preserved tower houses. At the top of the tower is a loggia , an open walkway more commonly found in the warmer climates of Italy and Spain, and provides a stunning panorama of the surrounding countryside. Hidden behind the tower are attractive terraced gardens where the Campbells could walk and enjoy the views.

One fine spring day I took Monkeydog to explore Dollar and Castle Campbell.

The most dangerous road in the 'Wee County' of Clackmannanshire is the road east from Tillicoultry (on the A91). It is a twisting road, known as the 'Dollar Bends.' The council reduced the speed limit on the Dollar Bends to 50 mph after much campaigning by the locals. It was a pointless exercise. The winding road makes it difficult to drive faster than the speed limit. Only trained traffic officers and reckless youths do so. I have been a passenger to both.

As a teenager my best friend drove me through the bends in his classic Austin Mini, a nimble motor capable of hugging the road like it was on rails. It probably felt faster than it really was. Then, on route to an emergency call, a traffic officer drove me through the Dollar bends in a powerful Volvo, it felt like we were on two wheels for most of the way. It was autumn and there were many wet leaves on the road. Despite clinging to my door handle for dear life, it comforted me that this highly trained officer knew what he was doing. When we arrived in Dollar, he said, 'Well that was lucky, sometimes you have to take a chance, eh!' I never got in the car with him again.

The Dollar Bends is Clackmannanshire's most dangerous road because it has taken many lives, including that of a golfing star just two weeks before his 18th birthday, a fireman on route to an emergency call and many more.

In the middle of the two mile stretch of bends is *Tait's Tomb* a walled burial ground for the Tait family who owned much of the surrounding land. The tomb has been untended for so long that trees have sprouted within its walls, one fir towers high inside and has grown so wide it fills the mausoleum. It is the twist in the road at Tait's Tomb that is the most dangerous. So dangerous locals say something haunts it. I know a witch hides in the trees there, I have seen her. Park up in the lay-by there and scan the woods on the opposite side of the road and you will see her too.

People have sighted apparitions at the tomb from as far back as the first world war. A bus driver saw a man, wearing a strange outfit, standing by the side of the road. He stopped and allowed him to board. Without a word spoken, the gentleman got on the bus and sat down. The driver started his engine and looked in his mirror to check on his passenger but he could not see him. He got up and searched the bus - it was empty. The driver searched outside, but the road was deserted, the only noise coming from an owl hidden in the trees. Shaken, he drove quickly to Dollar and the safety of the lamp lights.

Is the road cursed or is it simply notorious for being a devil to navigate at speed? It would seem to be prudent to straighten the road out. A little investment might save lives. However, this is not possible. The estate owners decreed that the road should meander through the land just like a river. I fancy they thought it would be a much more pleasant drive. A decision that has cost many lives.

The road is a favourite of boy racers. It allows them to test their handling skills and put their cars to the edge of their capabilities. It does not matter to them whether the speed limit is fifty or sixty. I admit in my police book (*The really funny thing about being a cop*) that local officers used to time themselves through the Dollar Bends whenever they had an emergency call to go to. I too have tried it. Once I navigated my way through the bends on the way to an alarm call. I timed myself but I can't say it was impressive, others were much more proficient. As I entered Dollar, I slowed to 30 mph, then as I turned into the main street I had to avoid a cat that scampered across my path, in doing so I mounted the kerb burst a tyre and suddenly a lamp post came in the car with me.

I am much more careful these days.

Before walking to Argyll's castle I stopped for a coffee. The few shops there are in Dollar are very nice. *Dollar's Deli* is full of unusual culinary delights from all over the world. I looked longingly in the window then headed on. *The Paper Shop* is on one corner of Bridge Street and from there I looked up to the hills to see my eventual destination. Castle Campbell thrusts out of the trees, broody and theatrical.

Half way along Bridge Street at No. 54 is an abandoned white building that now has a beautiful array of weeds spurting out of its gutters. This used to be The *Dollar Arms Hotel* and was a lively place serving beer, wine, whisky, and entertainment in the form of music and dance. Many decades ago, the local bobbies would come along at midnight and eject the patrons, sending them on their way home. Just as soon as they did, the police ducked back in again and sampled the delights served up by Phyllis, the publican, in what is known as a 'lock-in.' Many an officer left the pub three sheets to the wind. Drinking on duty was commonplace back then but police have become a much more professional organisation. Nowadays, if an officer is caught drinking on duty they would be sacked.

As a young police officer Dollar was part of my beat. The town had a vibrant personality. It supported a good selection of hotels and taverns. People travelled from far afield to partake of a pint and some banter. Dollar was a popular place that buzzed with heady excitement, like the first barbecue of summer. Over the years, one by one, the hostelries closed. Casualties of changing habits and tourists going elsewhere.

Sitting on an uncomfortable wooden bench outside a coffee shop on the main street running through the village, I looked across the road at *The King's Seat,* the last remaining pub in the town, named after one of the most visible peaks linking Tillicoultry to Dollar. It is a cracking little bar serving reasonably priced beer, and good beer at that. *Schiehallion* craft lager, named after a popular munro near Kinloch Rannoch, is brewed by the local *Harviestoun Brewery.* Harviestoun Brewery make the most interesting beers: *Ola Dubh* (black oil), *Bitter and Twisted* and *Old Engine Oil,* Great names for beer and well worth a taste. Forget the prima donna brewers if you have the opportunity try Harviestoun's delicious offerings, *The King's Seat* serves them all.

A poster in the window advertises a £5 curry on Wednesday nights. What's not to like? Good beer and a curry is a staple we should enjoy at least once a month. Yet, the King's Seat may be struggling. The last upholder of ale houses in Dollar is showing signs of neglect, the 'g' in the sign above the door has fallen off. And it has been like that for some time. It will be such a shame if this pub closes too. Can it survive selling food so cheap?

It was in Dollar that Captain John McNabb was born, raised into a poor family. John left his beloved Dollar home as a young boy and took to the sea. A career choice out of necessity. He didn't let his deprived upbringing hinder his desire. John worked his way up through the ranks and made his fortune as a shipowner - much of his money attributable to the slave trade, which wasn't abolished until thirty years after his death in 1802. In his will Captain John McNabb bequeathed half of his estate to fund a school for the parish of Dollar and shire of Clackmannan.

The trustees, followed his wishes and conceived of a great academy that would educate the boys and girls of Dollar parish. Thus Dollar Academy, founded in 1818, has become the oldest Co-educational boarding school in the United Kingdom.

Dollar Academy has a single 70-acre campus edged on the one side by pretty rows of Georgian houses and on the other by an 18-hole golf course. The main building is a striking neo-classical design by the eminent Scottish architect William Henry Playfair.

I sipped my second coffee and munched on a piece of carrot cake when a stream of blue blazers and tartan skirts poured out of the side streets onto the main thoroughfare signalling break time at the school. The pupils disappeared into the various shops like meerkats sighting an eagle. The street went quiet again. Safety assured, the blue blazers and tartan skirts emerged one by one, gorging themselves on pastries and whatever sugary fare they couldn't get at school. The flood of young people now lolled around in a puddle, fixated on their food. It occurred to me there was something different about these students. This was no ordinary school lunchtime, these kids engaged each other in conversation as they ate. Chatting, smiling and laughing. Something was different. I couldn't put my finger on it at first. It reminded me of the time I was at school. When we used to gobble food quickly so we could play football. It wouldn't have been the first time I saw a goalkeeper dive to save a ball with a half a sandwich in one hand and the other half in his mouth. The difference, I realised, was the lack of mobile phones. Any other lunchtime in any other school, pupils spend every break immersed in their phones - and they call it 'social media.'

Here in Dollar the students held their heads upright, they busied themselves in chat - a testament to how good a school Dollar Academy must be.

With sufficient caffeine in my system to undertake the walk up the glen I set off passing the abandoned and derelict Castle Campbell Hotel once owned by Alan Longmuir of Bay City Rollers fame. In the 1970s the Bay City Rollers enjoyed huge success at home and abroad with their distinctive tartan outfits and upbeat pop tunes such as Bye, Bye, Baby and Shang-A-Lang. They had a massive teen following, which included my older brother.

My big brother was my hero. He could make me laugh or cry at will. A protector who'd shield me from harm's way. He wouldn't let a soul bully me - that was his job. His ambition was to become the king of entrepreneurs and he did. A shining example to follow. I was in awe of my older brother. But when he came home at thirteen dressed in a Bay City Rollers outfit; massive flared trousers with a tartan stripe down the side and an unbuttoned tartan edged waistcoat, I just thought 'what a twat.'

A burn runs through the town passing by the Castle Campbell Hotel. Monkeydog and I walked along its grassy bank. Halfway up is the pretty stone building of Burnside House. It has a sprawling garden and ivy clambering up the walls all the way to the second floor. It has a plaque on the front celebrating councillor Lavinia Malcolm, who lived there from 1883 to 1910. She was the first woman provost in all of Scotland, taking up the position on Dollar Town Council in 1907 and served right through the Great War. Considering women didn't get an equal vote with men until 1928 you have to think this must have been a hard gig for her - so I tip my hat to Lavinia.

At the top of East Burnside is Dollar Golf Club, green fees can be paid at the bar - if closed you can leave your money in the honesty box. Like a lot of golf clubs across the country Dollar struggled to keep a decent membership and was in danger of folding. Everywhere else the clubs increased their membership fees to help stay afloat. This put people off who couldn't afford it.   The Dollar Golf Club committee took a different approach. One of their major costs was paying land rent. They negotiated with their landlord and got a large reduction in their payments. Where every other course in Scotland increased fees to meet their obligations, Dollar Golf Club reduced their fees by a whopping £100. A full membership is now nearly half that of other clubs in the county.

It is a decent course and unusual in that, dictated by the terrain, it has no bunkers. The most memorable hole is the second which is less than 100 yards but a blind shot to an elevated green. Get it wrong and it will cost you. The information about the honesty box finishes with a reminder to 'Pay up and play fair.' At only £15 for a round of golf there shouldn't be an issue, should there?

Next to the clubhouse is *The Dollar Museum*. Dollar Museum advertises itself as the perfect place to discover more about Dollar's history. It has a variety of exhibitions, a reading room, archives and photographs. I am sure it would all be very fascinating, but, at 10.30 a.m. on a Tuesday morning I was a little early for it to be open. I was, in fact, four days and 30 minutes too early. The Dollar Museum only opens at weekends and even then only from 11 a.m. to 4.30 p.m. I was disappointed. In the window was a poster advertising a new exhibition on *Adam Robson* a Scottish rugby internationalist. The picture of him caught my attention. He had a lived-in face, creased like a morning duvet. His battered shapeless ears protruded out the side of his head at different angles to each other but there was a glint in his eyes that hinted at intelligence.

Adam Robson had a distinguished rugby career. He was the first president of the Scottish Schools Rugby Union in 1967 and worked his way up to become president of the Scottish Rugby Union in 1984. In that year, with Robson at the helm, Scotland won their first Grand Slam since 1925. Passionate about rugby he was keen to 'put something back in.' Robson was equally passionate about his day job, that of an art teacher. He studied at Edinburgh College of Art and taught at Kirkcaldy Academy before becoming head of art at Dollar Academy. An accomplished artist himself, he sold many hundreds of works in his lifetime.

Robson died on 16 March 2007 aged 78. The next day the Scottish rugby team were playing France at the

Stade de France. In that famously intimidating cauldron the players and supporters fell silent to pay their respects to him. A fitting tribute for a passionate and dignified man. A man with an interesting face and an intelligent sparkle in his eye.

I saw a weathered and faded metal plaque on the door of the museum, secured with two rusty headed screws. It advised that entry is possible by arrangement, providing a six digit home number with no area code. I imagined a keen curator arriving to open up and show me around but having to spend an hour or two for the inconvenience. I wasn't convinced there would be someone on the other end of the line, anyway. I refrained from making the call. I had Monkeydog with me and we were there to walk. Between the Museum and the golf club is a path leading to Dollar Glen, we set off to explore.

The path opens out onto a grassy area with the burn on the left. Water tumbles downhill effortlessly, frothing and gurgling as it navigates the many boulders in its path. The grassy area is a favourite spot of the local dog owning housewives. They stood in a huddle, blethering away, oblivious as one of their dogs approached me, jumped up and left two dirty paw prints on my trousers. I gave it a dog treat to chew on whilst it contemplated the seriousness of its actions, but I don't think it cared. Monkeydog and I strode on. I hoped there would be no more dirty paw prints and Monkeydog hoped I didn't give away all his treats.

At the end of the grassy patch the path splits into two. A handy sign shows how the path takes an oval-shaped route around the Castle Campbell or Castle Gloom as I prefer. Castle Gloom is a much more evocative name, don't you think?

We took the clockwise route and after a steep ascent the path emerged next to the highest green on Dollar Golf Club. It had been years since I had played the course; I stopped for a breather and took in the rich views. I remembered it as a spectacular course to experience although you could do with climbing boots instead of golf shoes. I'd have stood for longer and admired the rolling countryside below but a chill wind forced me onwards and upwards.

Moments later I came across a tree stump. Someone had taken the time to haul a chainsaw up the steep slope and shape the stump into a toadstool. Hundreds of coins had been forced halfway into the hood then hammered flat on the outside, so it was hard to even distinguish their denomination. The light filtered through the trees and the coins glittered giving it an Alice in Wonderland look. There was nothing to suggest who had sculpted the stump or why. A pleasant oddity for a passing hiker.

The path meandered higher over some rough ground. Rounding a bend the landscape opened up and for the first time since Cairnpark Street I caught sight of Castle Campbell and it filled me with foreboding. It loomed ominous through the trees across the gorge, like a storm-cloud threatening a downpour. It deserves the name of Castle Gloom.

The path turned sharp left, and I wondered how it would lead me to the castle, there is no obvious route. I rounded another bend, and as if someone flicked a switch, I heard the crash of water in the gully below. I coame across a gated path to my right, and a sign advised it led to Windyedge Viewpoint. I opened the gate and Monkeydog raced through the pile of fallen leaves. Despite a metal fence separating the path from the ravine below I wasn't reassured of his safety. He disappeared out of sight too quick for my liking and I whistled, Monkeydog rejoined me at my side obedient as ever. The rocky descent is reminiscent of a scene from Jurassic Park. Stepping carefully I reached the viewpoint. The water cascaded over shelves of flat rock and twisted left disappearing into towering cathedral sized gaps chiselled through the stone. Monkeydog and I gaped in awe.

It crossed my mind this would be as good a place as any to dump a body - so be mindful of who you visit with.

Retracing our steps to the gate and rounding the side basin of the gully the path brought us out below Castle Gloom. A naturally defended position it has been impregnable since being built in the 15th Century. Although it has passed through many hands, it is now in the care of Historic Scotland.

There is a single track road all the way up to the Castle Campbell entrance. A car park is situated about 200 yards before you get there, below Brewlands Cottage on the other side of the gully. The Boy Scouts used Brewlands Cottage for many years as a base for their adventures. I recall spending a night there in my youth, roughing it in a sleeping bag on the cold floor, not getting much sleep and then being fed scrambled egg from a massive pot in the morning, it was horrible. Character building or torture? It was twenty years before I could face the taste of scrambled egg again.

I continued my clockwise route and descended the east side of the burn. It is easier going but still not for the infirm or faint-hearted. One minute the path leads you to the water, then the burn drops away and peering over the rickety fence down below is to be avoided by those suffering vertigo.

After my fourth or fifth cheery greeting to hikers on their way up, I realise I am in a good mood. A state of being requiring less effort than that of a bad mood. Mood is a choice. We can smile or we can frown. Moping takes effort and induces lethargy. Happy people get up and get on. They get out and about. They take an interest. Unhappy people sit and fester. Avoid them at all costs. Their mood is as infectious as the common cold. You won't meet unhappy people walking Dollar Glen in the company of a dog.

When I was a little boy I recall saying, 'Wow!' quite a lot. Stunned by the magic of nature in many forms. For many that feeling of wonder wanes as we get older. Holding onto that sensation is one of the most positive things we can do. No matter what life throws at you there will always be something that can make you say, 'wow' - the kid with the voice of an angel, the derring-do of a circus performer, the skill of a magician, the beauty in a flower, the strength of the sea, the majesty of a mountain or even just Monkeydog wagging his tail, happy to have come on an adventure.

Chapter eleven

THE HUNT FOR LOCH LEVEN'S LARDER

There are two lochs in Scotland which go by the name of Loch Leven. Loch Leven, the sea loch on the West Coast and Loch Leven, a freshwater body of water in the middle of Fife.

I had an inkling I would like to visit Loch Leven in Fife to find Loch Leven's Larder. I had seen the signposts for it when passing through Kinross and imagined it would be a nice place for a coffee and maybe it had a farm shop attached. It was the height of summer, I put Monkeydog in the back seat of my old motor, number one son in the front seat and made our way there. I fancied a nice walk by the loch and maybe a coffee and a sandwich for lunch. I estimated a forty-minute drive.

I shall reserve the right to ponder life's big questions on a drive: Who am I? Where did we come from? What is the meaning of our existence? What happens when we die? Is life an illusion? If God is truly all powerful why did he make me an atheist?

In the midst of these thoughts number one son turned to me and in all seriousness asked, "Dad, do monkeys eat chocolate?"

I took my eyes off the road to look at him, "I had the opportunity to give you up for adoption you know."

And they say children are our future!

We arrived at Milnathort having taken the wrong route by skirting the east side of the Ochil Hills. I had a vague idea of which direction we should head but, to make sure, I asked number one son to put it in the sat nav. It came back with a route that said we were forty-four miles away and it would take an hour. Something was wrong. Loch Leven's Larder couldn't have been more than two or three miles from us.

I wondered if the sat nav had mixed up the location.

"Did you put in the correct location?" I said calmly, trying hard to hide my irritation.

"Yes, Scotland's Larder, that's what it says."

Fortunately I didn't express my annoyance because I later discovered I had been wrong. It was my fault. I had been calling it Scotland's Larder instead of Loch Leven's Larder. Another good reason why getting angry can backfire.

I used my inferior manly sense of direction and carried on down country roads hoping that at some point I'd come out at Loch Leven, or at least see a signpost.

It pays to do your homework. Doing your homework is all important in getting to where you want to go in life. Not doing your homework invariably means taking a roundabout route. If you know where you want to get to then it makes sense to study and prepare. Not doing your homework means you sometimes take the wrong turning and instead of ending up at your goal you end up in a car park in the forest. My lack of preparation and my faulty sense of direction took me to the *'Burleigh Car Park.'* A Scottish Tourism Thistle information sign told me I had arrived at Loch Leven National Reserve and Heritage Trail. Not the part of the loch I'd intended, but it would do.

We parked up and got out. After a short walk we ended up at the loch side. The Heritage Trail is a thirteen mile path around Loch Leven. The path is flat and suitable for walkers, runners and cyclists. We went anti-clockwise, heading back towards Kinross.

It is a perfectly pleasant walk with stunning views across to the smaller island where Loch Leven Castle sits. Loch Leven Castle is one of the oldest castles in Scotland, built in the 1300s, a tall tower house dominates the ruins. Many famous characters visited the little island stronghold, including Robert the Bruce. They also used the castle to imprison Mary Queen of Scots.

Mary Queen of Scots, now she had a good start in life, at just six-days old she ascended the throne and became Queen of Scotland. In those days religion played a big part in political life, even for the monarchy. The Catholics didn't like the Protestant reformers and vice versa (nothing has much changed).

There was something about Mary the Protestants didn't like. Probably, they didn't like her trying to negotiate a Catholic marriage with Don Carlos son of Philip II of Spain. It didn't work out. In the process Mary put everyone's nose out of joint.

Conscious of the benefits of an alliance with France, instead Mary married the heir to the French Throne, Francis II, when he was 14 years-old and Mary 16, *there was definitely something about Mary*. Francis was not an academic, preferring hawking and horse riding to education. Unlike Mary who enjoyed her studies and loved to write poetry. Francis II ascended the throne at fifteen when his father died in a jousting accident. A year later he too was dead, an ear infection they say. Perhaps he didn't like Mary's poetry - who knows?

Five years later Mary married her first cousin, Lord Darnley, causing both the Catholics and the Protestants to screw up their faces like they had just sucked on a lemon. You can please some of the people some of the time but Mary Queen of Scots couldn't please anyone any of the time. She didn't even please her second husband (Lord Darnley). Their marriage soured and Mary turned to her Italian secretary, David Rizzio, for reassurance and guidance (read into that what you will).

This is sounding like an awful olden times soap opera.

It got worse.

The Protestant lords disliked Mary's dalliance with the Italian, they accused him of being a papal agent and too intimate with Mary. Egged on by Lord Darnley, who was still Mary's husband, the lords murdered Rizzio in her presence. Frightening times for Mary, considering she was six months pregnant.

I'm guessing Rizzio, the Italian gigolo, might have had more than just a hand in that.

On 19th June 1566 Mary gave birth to her son James (later to become James I of England). Later that year, with her marriage to Lord Darnley on the rocks, Mary befriended James Hepburn, Earl of Bothwell. Mary Queen of Scots looked for a way to dissolve her marriage with Lord Darnley. It wasn't long before the script writers of this drama threw in another shocker.

In February 1567, someone murdered Lord Darnley in circumstances that remain a mystery. The house in Edinburgh, where he was lodging, blew up. Yet, his body was found in the garden, and he had been strangled. The Earl of Bothwell was tried for Darnley's murder and acquitted after a brief trial.

I have thirty years of policing under my belt and I now have a natural inclination to question unusual happenstance. So when they say Mary Queen of Scots wasn't likely to have anything to do with the murder of her husband I raise an eyebrow. Just a quizzical look that says 'wait a minute.' Mary's dad died the week before she was born, her first husband, Francis II, died two years into their marriage. Lord Darnley, her second husband murdered her lover David Rizzio then Lord Darnley died in mysterious circumstances. Call it any way you like, the woman was a bloody jinx.

Mary was criticised for playing golf too soon after the death of her husband. So if they thought that was bad they were really miffed when she married Bothwell just weeks later. The Scots lords went to war with her army, she lost. On her surrender they imprisoned her in Loch Leven Castle. Bothwell fled and later died in Denmark, apparently insane.

If you are looking for tangled webs on which to weave a story, then you need look no further than the history books, I think.

Looking at Loch Leven Castle I wondered how a mollycoddled woman like Mary Queen of Scots managed to escape. She must have had support because once she got out she rallied another army to fight the nobles who imprisoned her. Luck wasn't on her side and she was once again defeated, this time at the Battle of Langside. She escaped to England where she was promptly locked up again. They threw away the key and two decades later she died, still in incarceration.

I related the Mary Queen of Scots story to Number one son and he was trapped - in the same way all young adults are when they haven't got an internet connection. As we walked the path, both my companions gave me a pleading look. One looking for a doggie treat and the other looking for me to shut up.

We admired the scenic little island on which the ruin of Loch Leven Castle stood and we enjoyed the wildlife that flitted about. We saw an osprey patrol the loch in search of a fish supper. The path around the loch has little wooden bridges, every so often, to help navigate through the rich mix of wet grassland, raised bogs and marshy edges. The route we took skirted Kinross Golf Club to the right and through the trees we could see the occasional group of golfers enjoying a pleasant round. There are two courses there giving thirty-six holes of golf to play if you are interested. The path took us out to a headland and then made a sharp turn back on itself. I was throwing a ball for Monkeydog, who chased after it with zeal but was less enthusiastic about bringing it back. Then Number one son wrestled it from him and threw it for him to chase. It was a shame, Monkeydog loved that ball.

#1soncannythrowaballtosavehimself.

We stood on a bench to look over a wall to see the intriguing Kinross House & Gardens. Kinross House & Gardens was built in the late-seventeenth century by Sir William Bruce and was once described as the coldest house in Scotland, having only four radiators to heat a house which can cater for up to twenty-eight overnight guests. It has since been renovated and looks positively delightful. It used to be open to the public, but it is now in private hands and used for weddings and events. It has one and a half square miles of walled grounds. Looking through the entrance archway the stately mansion sits at the end of a mile long driveway which skirts around a picturesque fountain. The grounds, which has a helipad, coach house and spa, are meticulously maintained. We could only admire it from afar. I do intend, one day, to drive my old motor up that driveway, around the fountain and stop at the main entrance where I will ask if I can go and get my Monkeydog's ball back.

The trail around Loch Leven opens out at the approach to Kinross. A large area is set aside for grass and the occasional bench. The council keep it in good order. We followed the path as close to the water as we could and arrived at the small harbour. By necessity they have put in a raised wooden path through the reeds and marsh. There are several interesting signposts and artwork around Loch Leven that enhance the experience of walking the Heritage Trail. Loch Leven brims with natural beauty, wildlife and history. The RSPB have a nature reserve on the loch and it is no surprise; the area teems with a great variety of birds. It is a unique environment attracting not only the largest concentration of breeding ducks in the UK, but many thousands of migratory ducks, geese and swans every autumn and winter. You can imagine the din in autumn as 20,000 pink-footed geese fly in from Iceland. Loch Leven brown trout, prized for their pink flesh, have been sent to stock waters all over the world. Before climate change brought in milder weather, curling tournaments called 'bonspiels' were held on the loch when it was covered in thick winter ice.

We came across a small wooden bench. In ornate writing, engraved onto the side were the utterly charming words:

'Wee gallus quackies hae bonnie feasties oan
snails and flees and wee black beasties'

131

We carried on through the marshes and came out at the harbour. There is a small tourist shop where you can buy a boat trip across to Castle Island. There was a queue forming on the jetty. Had I known about it I might have taken the trip, at £7.50 a head it didn't seem too expensive. I'd need to check they would take my four-legged friend first. There is quirky *Boathouse Bistro* at the back of the tourist shop, and the *Coffee Shop* with a decked area overlooking the loch. It allowed us to sit outside and partake of coffee and savoury crepes. Crepes are normally served with a variety of sweet fillings so I was interested to try the pesto and rocket. Number one son chose a spicy tortilla and tomato. It was a nice day to be sitting outside, with bonnie views and good company. The coffee was good and the savoury crepes were hot and delicious.

We had a pleasant walk back to the car and a scenic drive home. I promised myself I'd go back again and see if I could find Loch Leven's Larder.

I didn't make the trip again until winter. One cold but dry Sunday I headed off in the car with Monkeydog in the back but this time with Mrs McEwan sitting up front. Instead of going up and around the Ochil Hills I cut across country, convinced I knew where I was going. Once again I came unstuck. We had a pleasant enough drive but this time I arrived just short of Kelty. Mrs McEwan inserted Loch Leven's Larder into the sat nav and it was directing us to join the motorway north. I wasn't convinced. I could see Loch Leven just the other side of Kelty and it would have made sense to carry on through the town and find it that way. However, we were hungry and had just passed *Baxter's*

Restaurant, Deli and Shop. I turned around, and we went in there for lunch.

Baxters is Scotland's most famous soup maker. The restaurant and grounds were very nicely kept and there were photogenic Heilan Coos (Highland Cows) in the adjacent fields. Several tourists were out with their cameras by the fence taking pictures. The Heilan Coos obliged by turning their hairy horned heads towards them and posing moodily. They are such cracking beasts.

The restaurant itself was clean and modern. Large windows gave views across to the Pentlands. There was outside seating, but it was too cold for them to be in use. The restaurant had obviously been busy, and it was now 2 p.m., which is why I will excuse some of the service we received, but not all. The waiter ignored us for a bit, he looked grumpy and stressed. When he did eventually show us to a seat, he was unsmiling and monosyllabic.

"Two?"

"Yes please," and he waved us to follow him.

He showed us to a two-seater table by the window. The restaurant was still half full of customers finishing their meals. A group of ten grey haired women's guild members were causing a disturbance at the table in the middle - in that loud way crinkly women do when they can't remember what they ordered and protest they will never be able to eat all the chips that came with their food.

"Menu?" said our grumpy waiter as he handed it over.

I took the menu from him and he walked off.

A minute later he returned, took out his pad and asked us for our order with the one word, "Ready?"

I didn't need much to eat, but here we were in Baxter's restaurant and it would seem rude not to try their soup. I hadn't quite decided what else to have, "Could you give us a minute more, please?"

"Sure," he said and walked off never to darken our table again.

Ten minutes later, I managed to attract the eye of a younger waiter with a wave. There were two soups on the menu, so we ordered one of each, a sandwich and a glass of water. The food arrived and I have to say, as you would expect, the soup was delicious. Not only that, the sandwiches were on a light brown, fresh bread. Top marks for presentation and taste.

The waiter forgot the water, so I attracted his attention and asked again. He arrived back with two glasses, these were unceremoniously slammed onto the table with such a thunk that some water jumped up and spilled over. The young lad turned away so fast I said, 'thank you,' to the back of his head.

The secret to remaining calm in these circumstances is not to get upset, but get revenge. The simplest retribution for bad service is to not give a tip. The food was excellent, it had stunning views but the service smudged our dining experience. That service went unrewarded. We left the restaurant and made our way into the deli. With the money I saved on the tip I bought three tins of soup which I very much enjoyed for lunch over the next week. Revenge, it turns out, is a dish best served piping hot in a bowl with some buttered toast.

Sometimes life can be a pain in the neck. It becomes too much; we get stressed, and it affects our mood. Waiters get cranky, we all can. That is often to our detriment. It might cost us a tip. It might cost us future business or a promotion. Even worse, it might cost us our life.

When we view stress as a bad thing it is detrimental to our health. When we get stressed the little processor in our brain sends out an order: Release the stress hormones! These are the same hormones that trigger our body's 'fight or flight' response. Our heart races, our breath quickens, and our muscles tense in readiness for action. When that happens too regularly it puts our health at risk. It weakens our immune system, causes insomnia, gives us high blood pressure and increases the risk of a heart attack. But there is a way to deal with it.

Dealing well with the pressures of life requires us to change our mindset about stress. Instead of seeing it as a bad thing we should look upon it as a positive. We should recognise that it is our body preparing us to meet the challenge, it is preparing us for action. Seeing it as a helpful response is as simple as recognising the symptoms and saying 'Oh look, I am excited.' Recognising the release of our stress hormone has prepared our body to do anything negates the anxiety we might otherwise feel. Viewing stress as helpful works against the bad influence it has on our bodies. Selflessness is one of the best ways to reduce the affects of stress. Caring creates resilience. So no matter what walk of life you are in, if someone is causing you stress then you should go out of your way to be nice to them. If you are a waiter, remember the water and put it down on the table with a smile.

We got back in the car, took direction from the sat nav and took off down the motorway. Had I followed my nose earlier through Kelty and headed for the loch at the other side I would have ended up not at Loch Leven but at

Loch Ore. I didn't find this out until later when I looked at the map. It wouldn't have been a disaster. Loch Ore is home to *Lochore Meadows Country Park* and looks interesting enough to put on my list of places to visit.

We left the motorway at Fruix and took an anticlockwise direction around Loch Leven. We passed the RSPB Nature Reserve, which looked too busy for our liking, and carried on to Loch Leven Lodges, but that was even busier. I returned to the road and was surprised when a police car passed.

They are an unusual sight these days.

This marked police car was different, though, it was an American muscle car. I wasn't aware the Scottish Police used those cars. I wasn't even sure of the make, just that it looked big and mean. I drove up behind it to see if I could identify what it was. I followed it for three miles until it turned off in the village of Scotlandwell. By that time I had identified it as a 410 bhp V8 Ford Mustang. The decision to use the Ford Mustang by the Scottish Traffic Police is based on the affordable performance it provides and for high speed pursuits. Not a bad decision in terms of cost, just as long as those high speed pursuits are in a straight line. American muscle cars may be fast but they are not renowned for their ability to take corners. For your information, Scotland's roads are not famed for being long and straight.

I carried on through Scotlandwell and Kinneswood on the A911. Turned left at Balgeddie Toll Tavern and lo-and-behold *Loch Leven's Larder* appeared on my left. I turned in happy to have found it, although annoyed at myself for having already eaten. My annoyance was replaced with relief. The place was mobbed. I had to wait on cars leaving to gain entry to the car park and finding a free spot wasn't easy. I was about to turn around and drive out again when I spotted a signpost showing a path to the loch. That news pleased Monkeydog - a walk at last - he wagged.

We followed the path around the outskirts of the car park and that took us to the rear. There is a decked area and garden tables dotted around. Two giant glass pods sat on a decked area and I noted a family eating in one and a young couple canoodling over coffee in the other. The pods are a nice touch. As is the play park for the kids, several adults were there and appeared to be having as much fun as their children.

We followed the path half a mile down to Loch Leven and on to the Heritage Trail. We walked anti-clockwise and would have come to the Burleigh Car Park if we had kept going. Instead we admired the sunset, took pictures and toddled back to our car making polite remarks to everyone who crossed out path. I might go to the Burleigh Car Park again, take a clockwise route around the loch and stop for a coffee at Loch Leven's Larder. It would be a pleasant thing to do on a dry day any time of the year.

I have since been back to Loch Leven's Larder. From the front, Loch Leven's Larder looks like a converted hay barn, cold and cheap. Don't let that put you off, inside it was warm and friendly. Good food and excellent service. Which is why it has survived and Baxters hasn't. Baxters served great food but we don't like grumpy waiters, people voted with their feet and the restaurant closed.

The thing is; there is not just something about Mary, there is something about all of us. We circle around this thing we call life and stop off at places meet people and it is all random. We cross paths with others and sometimes our experiences aren't good and sometimes they are absolutely brilliant. But we never know until we try. We can set ourselves goals in life and if we concentrate on them, we will end up where we want to be. If I had set the sat nav properly or did my homework, I'd have found loch Leven's larder first time. Satisfied with getting to where I wanted to go. I didn't. I had a different experience; I found places I didn't know were there, and they were delightful. I was glad I had no sense of direction on this occasion. My alternative route gave me a brighter experience. One I have shared. Experience allows me to choose my future goals with the benefit of that knowledge.

It made me think. This is something I can apply to all aspects of my life. If I have the time, I shouldn't be precious about it. I should explore, I should try new restaurants, taste local delicacies, wander aimlessly until I happen upon things that take my interest. If I don't, I should pick the best experience and do it again.

Chapter twelve

GUARANTEED TO CAUSE FALL OUT THE MORNING AFTER

I have a fondness for Aberdeen.

I spent a year in Aberdeen as a student, growing from a naïve teenager into an adult, although even now I'm still a little naive. Despite the cold, (Aberdeen is on a higher latitude than Moscow) I had a wonderful year experiencing all the delights of extra-curricular university activities. It was only a year because I spent too little time bothering with the curricular activities - much to my eternal shame.

Oil changed Aberdeen. The discovery of the giant Forties Oil Field saw a gush of oil companies flow to the area. It sparked an enormous demand for housing, hotels, new constructions, shipping, labour and new infrastructure. Aberdeen became the modern equivalent of the Klondike Gold Rush. Here the rush was for crude oil.

Forty years on and the Granite City boasts the highest concentration of millionaires in the UK. House prices and rent reflect this. A glance at any estate agency window will make you gulp. My concern is for those not involved in the oil industry, there is a definite divide between the haves and the have nots. A starkness to the inequality. The police talked about introducing a 'weighting' allowance for police officers in Aberdeen, similar to the London weighting the Metropolitan Police receive, to lure new officers to the North. It hasn't happened and Police Scotland continue to lose good police officers to the oil industry.

Police Scotland tried a different tactic. After completing their training at the Scottish Police College, twelve officers from the central belt were taken to one side and told they were to be posted to Aberdeen. The officers would need to uproot and head north. Family and friends were not a consideration. All twelve of the new recruits resigned.

My number one son was a student in Aberdeen and lives there now. Unlike me he completed his course. He spent his first year in halls of residence then moved into a flat with two friends. A grotty looking place that would make you gag - mostly at the price. Three boys sharing a flat who study all week and work weekends have little time for housework. When I visited I sat in the one place and didn't move, for fear of something crawly dragging me into its lair. We popped up to see him after the owner had refurbished the place.

"They have even replaced the linoleum in the kitchen," said his delighted flatmate.

We edged into the kitchen to have a look.

"Do the tiles still come up when you hoover it?" Number one son asked his flatmate.

"Hoover! HOOVER!" I roared in laughter, "Who are you trying to kid?"

I'm still not sure he knows what a vacuum cleaner is.

Last year I qualified for the Police Golf Championships held at *Newmacher Golf Club, Aberdeen*, which has two cracking courses. A group of us came up a day early for a practice round. Rather than go out with the guys at night I met up with number one son for a quiet meal. The golf guys would make it a late night and I wanted a good night's sleep in readiness for the competition the next day.

Number one son took me to a place called *The Orchid*, on Langstane Place, which runs parallel to Union Street. We opened the heavy inlaid wooden door and went in. A short staircase took us down to an enchanting bar. A waitress welcomed us and showed us to a comfy leather settee near the window. Table service for drinks, posh. Our waitress was as exotic as the surroundings, she had piercings and tattoos, blonde hair and a nice smile. Before making any order, she placed glasses on our table, filled them with water and then handed us a cocktail menu, a glance confirmed my fears, this place was expensive.

They only had three beers on offer, we had the choice of fruity, malty or complex. I ordered the fruit, number one son ordered the malty, and I agreed to swap with him if it wasn't to his liking.

The beer arrived. We stared at our drinks - expectations dashed. It wasn't the presentation, or the service, or the surroundings. What dejected us was the quantity. We both presumed we were to receive thirst quenching pints of beer, instead we got petite tulip glasses that were only half full. Little glasses from which I would use to sip port.

"Just a sec," I said to our waiter. I took my glass, had a sip, swirled it around my mouth as if I were sampling wine, I smiled, "yes that's fine, we'll take a bottle."

My sarcasm was rewarded with a smirk, she about turned and headed back to the bar.

"Geezy peeps, that's an expensive mouthful of beer. How often do you come here?" I asked number one son, concerned I was paying for his champagne lifestyle.

"I've never been in here before, Dad. It's too expensive. I always wanted to try it though and thought this was an ideal opportunity since you are paying."

Any indignation I had melted away when he burst out laughing. It is impossible to be angry at him when he laughs. We tasted each other's beer and within two or three gulps our glasses were empty.

"Let's go eat!"

I handed number one son a ten pound note, and he went off to the bar to pay for our drinks. I extricated my jacket from the back of my chair and put it on. On his return I put out my hand for the change.

"What?"

"Change!"

"Oh! I thought you meant me to leave it as a tip."

"A tip! Over seven quid for two miniscule beers and you want to leave a tip?"

"Well she was nice, and the service wasn't bad."

I did the maths in my head and winced. I turned back to the table and gulped my glass of water, anything to make it seem like I was getting value for my ten quid. I can be such a miserable sod at times.

The restaurant number one son took me to was excellent, serving tasty barbecued meats with homemade sauces. It was so lip smacking good I bought a jar of their spicy sauce to take home. Regretfully, the restaurant isn't there anymore. Why is it the moment I find a good restaurant it burns down, changes hands or the Environmental Health condemn the place?

After dinner, we weren't ready to call it a night so number one son took me for a nightcap. A little place called 'Six Degrees North,' the sign above the door written as *'six°north'*. If you are a craft beer enthusiast, then this is the place to go. They have around 350 beers to choose from. The bar had tap after tap along its length. So much choice I didn't know what to order - and this is the beauty of the place - they let you try before you buy. They have small taster glasses and allowed us a sip of each beer until we found one we liked. Number one son and I were both amused by this and without a word being spoken we gave each other a look that set down the challenge: how many beers could we try before we were so embarrassed we had to order.

I lost.

We ordered spicy nuts, also delicious, and sat down to sip our drinks. Soon we were back up at the bar swirling more tasters. What a great pub. After several trips to the bar (and toilet) I reminded number one son I was trying to have a sober evening.

"Well, you failed!"

"I know!" I paused for a moment, "Right, one last beer and we will go."

On the road back to my hotel he pointed out *'Siberia Vodka Bar'* on Belmont Street.

"Would you like a nightcap, Dad?"

"I don't mind if I do," and we dodged into what was a very busy pub for a Sunday night. There is a reason it was busy, they were having an open mic night. Singers squeezed themselves into the corner of a bar and entertained us with their music. It was so busy every time someone raised an elbow on the other side of the bar the ripple effect caused me to spill my drink.

"I like this place," I said, "just a pity we can't get a seat."

"I know another place near your hotel, it has even better live entertainment."

So off we went, up Union Street and down Bridge Street into *'The Bridge Street Social Club.'* Ignoring the upstairs bar, number one son took me down a flight of stairs to the entertainment. There was a small stage at one end where a hairy man strummed away on a guitar and sang a song I recognised but couldn't name. This is a particular trait of mine, I like music but am useless at singing. I invariably get the words mixed up, or worse the notes.

Number one son recognised friends near the stage, so we sat with them to enjoy the entertainment. I didn't have to move an inch, every so often I handed number one son some paper from my wallet and he appeared back with drinks for everyone. So much for my quiet night!

At one point the pretty redhead sitting next to me engaged me in conversation, she laughed at my jokes - which was all I needed to fall in love with her. My beer fogged brain wondered if she was interested in going out with number one son. Who wouldn't want your dad as a wing-man?

"So how long have you known number one son?"

"Who?"

"Number one son," I said pointing at him.

"I don't know him."

There was me thinking I was chatting with one of my son's university friends and all the time it was just some random girl. Laughing and joking with a beautiful young girl because I thought she was friends with my son. She wasn't, and I dreaded to think what she thought. Time I left.

Number one son poured me into my hotel about 2 a.m., no doubt satisfied he'd emptied my wallet, but it didn't matter, we had a great night.

On our latest family visit to Aberdeen we took a trip to Hazelhead Park on the western outskirts of the city. It was over thirty years since I had been there and I remember it having a great maze. The maze is still there, although I was disappointed to note how run-down it had become. Gaps in the hedge made it possible to cheat. Number one son brought his girlfriend with him and we challenged them to see who could make it to the flagpole in the centre first. They won. Two minutes into the challenge they were there. Mrs McEwan, Monkeydog and I would still be there yet if we hadn't climbed through the gap in a hedge. (Well, you try it, have a look on Google Earth and see how hard it is).

The park itself has pretty azalea and rhododendron borders. Full-time gardeners keep the heather beds pristine. Dotted around are interesting sculptures, cultural and heritage items. One path around the back of the maze has inscriptions chiselled into the stone. Things like:

Remembering An
Old Torry Loon
And A Shiprow Quine
Sixty Years Together

There were other romantic words here and there and it all add to the charm.

There are two gardens. The Queen Mother Memorial Garden, which is worth seeing in full bloom. The size of half a football pitch it has regimented borders filled with rose bushes. We visited in October so it was bare but pleasant none-the-less. A similar garden next to it is a memorial to all who died in the Piper Alpha disaster.

On 6th July 1988, a hundred miles offshore from Aberdeen a gas explosion caused a fire that destroyed the Occidental Oil Platform. The catastrophe killed 167 of the 228 workers on the rig. It remains the world's worst off-shore disaster.

The City of Aberdeen keep the Piper Alpha Memorial Garden in immaculate condition. Tended with care and not a thing out of place. We made our way to the commemorative statue in the centre. A ten feet high base supports three life-size oil workers in brass, each staring out in different directions. I imagined them seeking answers; why did this have to happen?

We quietened on our approach and as we circled the Memorial, reading the names and ages of all those who lost their lives, then we became silent. I read names of men who were no older than my son standing beside me. Inscribed on the south face of the Memorial plinth above the Celtic Cross are the names of the thirty men who have no resting place on shore. Interred behind the Cross is a casket of unknown ashes. On the east face of the plinth are inscribed the names of two heroic crewmen of the Sandhaven who made the supreme sacrifice for their fellow men. They tried to save the lives of others and in doing so lost their own.

Piper Alpha was once the biggest oil and gas producing platform in Britain. It brought in over 300,000 barrels of crude oil a day (10% of the country's total). A consortium of foreign companies owned Piper Alpha. Occidental, an American-based company, operated the platform on their behalf. In the 1980's the price of oil plunged from $30 a barrel to $8. Occidental scaled back their spending. The platform was originally designed to recover crude oil, but they made renovations so it could also take gas. Safety was compromised when gas compression units were installed next to the central control room. As part of the modifications, construction, maintenance and upgrade works began. Occidental took the decision to continue to recover oil and gas during these overhauls. They valued the bottom line over staff safety. The dangers ignored. Greed to the fore.

The inevitable happened. In a communication break-down at a change of shift, staff were not aware they should not use a key piece of pipework. Gas leaked out and ignited. Firewalls failed to cope with the explosion. The platform was completely destroyed, and it took Red Adair, the famed American wild well controller, three weeks to bring the fire under control.

The police had many difficulties during their enquiry into the disaster. First they had to recover the accommodation platform in which many of those oil workers died. The recovered module was docked upside down, which did not assist the investigation teams - it isn't easy climbing an upside down stairwell.

Following the extensive enquiry into the disaster, Lord Cullen judged Occidental had used inadequate maintenance and safety procedures. He made 106 safety recommendations for drilling in the North Sea. I would like to add my recommendation to make it 107. Visiting the Piper Alpha Memorial should be compulsory for all oil company executives. A prerequisite before getting a licence to operate. The Memorial serves as a fitting and sobering reminder that a voracious apetite for money can have tragic consequences.

Afterwards, number one son entertained us for lunch. When I say 'entertained,' I mean he amused us by making us pay for it.

He has good taste. Often we look for dog friendly places. The Long Dog Café in the West End being one. A quirky little spot that welcomes dogs - as long as they keep their owners on a lead. They have the most indulgent milk shakes I've ever tasted. If you don't mind dying young (and you won't when you savour these) then this is the place to go. They may rack up a few more points than your Weight Watchers diet allows in a week, but they are (literally) to die for.

This time he took us to *Cognito Delicatessen*. Cognito is one of the many coffee shops taking over from where corner shops used to be in the housing schemes of Aberdeen. Travel up Union Street from the sea and carry on past all the shops, then take a detour into any of the streets to your right or left and you will find similar interesting shops and cafes. They are much more pleasant than big chain coffee shops. They don't have the same queues, or the same rush to get you in and out. You don't pick a sandwich and then hand it over to get it toasted, they note your order on a pad from the comfort of your chair.

Cognito has four quirky tables by the window with comfortable padded leather bench seats and two chairs on the other side rescued from a cinema. They also have tall stools to sit on at the counter. And what a counter. Great big glass jars filled with Red Delicious apples that did indeed look red and delicious. Scrumptious cakes and pastries behind a glass case and little odds and ends scattered around: Nice beers, tasty looking cheeses, olives and much more. A big chalk board sign on a door at the far wall that said;

'This is Ben's office, where all the interesting stuff happens!'

The waiters smiled and went about their business efficiently and with an air of what they were doing was important. Even they were interesting, our waiter had his sleeves rolled up to reveal both arms bore striped patterned tattoos. Not garish, but tasteful like an expensive wallpaper. The smell from the coffee machines was enough to drag you in. I loved it.

I ordered a salmon and Creme Fraiche Bruschetta. While we waited on our food, I eyed up the plates being served to the other customers. Every single dish looked appetising, varying from tarts to toasties and piled with colourful salad. I would have eaten all of them - in the one sitting. Try to pinch anything off my plate and you risk being stabbed with a fork.

Afterwards, we walked off our lunch with a stroll along the beach, Monkeydog leading the way. From where we were, it is a three mile drive to the shore but it only took twelve minutes. I don't know of any other city in the world you could drive through their main street in so short a time.

Aberdeen has about a mile and a half of sandy beach that suffers from significant erosion so there are timber groynes every fifty yards, stretching out to the sea to help keep the sand from disappearing. An esplanade above the storm wall runs the full length of the beach and is used by runners, cyclists and dog walkers who can't be bothered with cleaning sand off trainers, bikes or wet mutts. We went straight to the beach. Number one son threw stones into the water, hoping Monkeydog would be stupid enough to follow it in and get soaked.

I noticed a group of people by the road changing into wetsuits, they grabbed surfboards and headed down to the water behind us. The sea looked calm and I wondered if they knew something I didn't.

It was a pleasant walk. After a while, number one son stood on a groyne and walked out to the sea until the waves were lapping just below his feet. He had a handful of stones in his hand. Monkeydog followed but stopped short of the wash. Number one son threw a stone over the groyne and Monkeydog, in his enthusiasm, chased after it vaulting the groyne. The other side was lower where the sand had washed away. On seeing a big wave come tearing up the side of the groyne, Monkeydog forgot all about the stone and tried to jump back up to safety. The wood was wet and slippy. Monkeydog's front paws scrambled to climb the groyne, he failed to gain purchase, and he fell back just as the wave crashed into him. Monkeydog tumbled upside down in the wash, much to the delight of number one son. The very next wave put paid to number one son's glee as it smashed into the post he stood on and ran over his legs up to his knees, splashing salty water up the left side of his body - much to the delight of his Mum and Dad.

The tide was coming in. The surfers did know something. The calm waters were replaced by big waves that hit the shore with increasing ferocity.

We turned around and headed back to the car. Just as well we did. Dark clouds billowed in from the northwest hurling rain down like a moving waterfall. We climbed into the car seconds before the rain fell in pellets, bouncing off the roof like it was a drum. Monkeydog sat in the back on his damp towel, smelling like a wet dog. Number one son sat in the front with drenched trousers, smelling even more like a wet dog than the dog. I waited on a gap in the traffic, put the windscreen wipers on full speed and headed off past *The Beach Ballroom*.

The Beach Ballroom used to sit all on its own. Now there is a swimming pool and ice rink next to it. Further south on the Esplanade are several independent cafes and bars. There is an amusement arcade, two small run-down cafes and a newer complex containing a cinema and several bog standard restaurants chains.

There used to be a nice bistro on the front. It had marble tables, comfy leather chairs, free newspapers, bacon rolls and smelled of cookies fresh from the oven. I often wandered down on a Sunday morning to while away a few hours. On one occasion Fraser, a law student joined me. Fraser was a patter merchant and womaniser. We spent a pleasant morning reading the news, eating bacon rolls, drinking coffee. While I completed the easy crosswords, Fraser went off to chat to girls and had a remarkable success rate in getting their phone numbers. As the morning gave way to afternoon Fraser returned to the table.

"Do you fancy a pie and a pint?"

"Sure, why not?"

I followed Fraser out the bistro, up to Union Street and then down to the docks. Aberdeen harbour cuts a mile into the heart of the city where tankers can shelter from the heartless North Sea. Fraser took me into a grotty looking little pub by the quay, I imagine it might still be there. It smelled of stale lager and corned beef. Scotland were playing East Germany in the European Football Championship qualifier. The pub advertised the game, a cheap pint of stout, a free pie and half-time entertainment in the form of a stripper. It was standing room only. Fraser and I guzzled pints of stout and bit our nails through a fraught first half of football. When would Souness be sent off? When would Archibald get injured? When would East Germany score?

At half-time the attention turned to the stripper. All heads turning 180 degrees from the television screen above the bar to the raised dais at the rear of the pub. Debbie (I think Debbie was her real name) stepped nervously onto the stage sporting a thick fur coat that extended to the floor. Peter Mayhew (the actor who played Chewbacca in *Star Wars*) later borrowed it for the role. Debbie did an amazing impression of an Inuit in a snowstorm for the first ten minutes. She clutched her fur coat tight to her body while swaying to the sounds of *Culture Club* as if it were minus fifty and even the slightest exposure of skin would give her frostbite. Eventually the fur coat dropped a little off her shoulders to reveal another layer of clothing that wouldn't get a Victorian age prospector excited. Debbie looked somewhat distraught as the crowd bayed for a little flesh - as promised by the advertising hoarding outside. I felt for her, I really did. Then Debbie plucked up the courage and the fur coat dropped to the floor, she had long black elbow-length gloves on. She pulled at each finger until first one glove then the other came off and they too dropped to the floor. The crowd cheered their first sight of flesh. Then it didn't matter, the second half started and every head turned 180 degrees back to the television, eyes glued to the game.

And what a game. Jock Stein had our boys fired up. Eight minutes into the second half John Wark scored. Our initial eruption abated and left us feeling more troubled than before. Elation gave way to trepidation. When would Souness receive his second yellow and be sent off? When would Archibald be stretchered from the pitch? When would East Germany get an equaliser and go on to score their winner?

Stein took Alan Brazil off in the 71st minute. It was an inspired substitution as his replacement, Paul Sturrock, scored just four minutes later. The atmosphere in the grotty little pub turned from one of trepidation to sheer unadulterated delight. I've seen less bouncy punk rock concerts.

At full time Debbie, now dressed in a revealing tank top and short skirt, had the job of dishing out the microwaved pies. We didn't care, we were on a high. We ate the soggy pies, downed more stout and went home thrilled. It took longer than it should have for me to realise I don't actually like watching strippers, eating microwaved pies, or drinking stout.

We killed an hour in *The Tollbooth Museum*. You can find it at the east end of Union Street attached to Aberdeen Sheriff Court. The museum used to be a jail in the 17th-century and is essentially preserved as it was then. It requires some agility to navigate the small spiral staircases, but it is worth the effort. There is a 'scold's gag' on display. A metal frame used as corporal punishment for women accused of slanderous talk and malicious gossip. The helmet fitted over the head with a metal tongue thrust into the mouth.

Mrs McEwan was not pleased when I asked an attendant if it was for sale.

I enjoyed reading the tales from the Tollbooth. One of the most common crimes was that of being a 'debtor.' Yet some of these debtors could afford to buy a key and come and go as they pleased.

Peter Williamson (or Indian Peter) was kidnapped as a boy from the harbour and incarcerated in the prison until they could sell him on as a slave. A common practice at the time and one which the authorities turned a blind eye. Like many such children, they sold Peter to a merchant and he was taken to America. After his master died, Peter married and settled on a farm in Pennsylvania. Native Americans attacked his farm and took him prisoner although badly tortured they kept him alive and then sold him to another tribe of Indians. This tribe kept him enslaved for a long time before he escaped. When he returned to his farm, he found his wife dead. With intent to seek revenge on the natives who tortured him, Peter joined the British Army, who were fighting a war with the French and the Indians. The army involved him in many battles and he saw many bloody massacres by the Indians, one being the famous surrender to the French and the events that the film *The Last of the Mohicans* made famous.

In the end, his regiment had to surrender. The French took him to Canada as a prisoner of war. There he became part of a prisoner exchange and on being set free he made his way back to Scotland. Back in Aberdeen he tracked down the men behind the slave trade. He publicly accused them and took them to court in a landmark case that exposed the scandal of slave trading. I believe Peter Williamson's life was the inspiration for *A Man Called Horse*.

A movie that, when mentioned, will always remind me of Richard Harris hanging by his nipples from ropes attached to wooden staves thrust through his skin.

Next we took a wander down to *Aberdeen Maritime Museum* at Shiprow, near the harbour. It is a lovely museum with many levels, nooks and crannies. There are interactive displays, paintings, incredible ship and boat models. There are educational themes where you can learn about the North Sea oil and gas industry. A café in the basement whet our whistle with coffee and filled our bellies with cake. My favourite piece is hidden away on one of the higher levels, up a staircase that goes nowhere but lean on the railing and you will see it hanging on the wall directly in front of you. And that piece will remain a mystery unless you visit.

The good thing about both the Tollbooth and Maritime Museums are they are free - albeit they welcome donations.

Number one son booked us a surprise restaurant for dinner. I figured it would be an expensive restaurant - it would have been a surprise if had taken us to a grotty little pub for a pie and a pint. We found *The Adelphi Kitchen* down a small close just off the bottom of Union Street. A small arched tunnel leading to it has the word 'ADELPHI' engraved in the stone above. The restaurant is a tiny place with only about ten tables. We sat at a table furthest away from the door but if the door was open, I could still have spat my chewing gum out onto the street.

Number one son explained his choice of restaurant. He is a good cook, his flatmates all take turns to cook every night, so they eat well. He asked me if I could cook what

155

they placed in front of me. I ordered the beef cheeks and admitted I wouldn't know where to start.

"That is why I like coming here," he explained, "I don't like to order something I can make myself. I feel cheated spending money on food I can cook just as good as a restaurant."

It was a reasonable explanation, but I took a mental note to query how, as a student, he could afford to eat in more expensive restaurants than we did. His mother got in before me.

"I understand, but how often are you eating in here?"

"Only once or twice a year, Mum. Just special occasions."

"Would those special occasions be when someone else is paying for it?" I said, adding my tuppence worth.

"Yeah, but it could be worse, Dad."

"How?"

"Well, it would be worse if I was paying," and he burst out laughing.

Number one son has such an infectious laugh, and he uses it to get on our good side. I can't not smile when he starts and invariably end up guffawing along with him like a demented hyena. His laugh is so contagious people at the table behind us joined in laughing too, and they hadn't a clue what they were laughing at.

I could be angry as hell with him, like the time he poured *Ribena* into my bottle of Barolo (the most expensive bottle of wine I ever purchased). He was only twelve. He looked at me, smiled and giggled, then his lungs opened up and he howled with laughter. I couldn't help myself, I shrugged my shoulders in defeat and let go with a great big belly laugh. The two of us snorting like our whole bodies were getting a massage. I swear, if number one son were ever in court, all he would need to do to get the jury on his side is grin at them and then explode into raucous laughter - they would disintegrate.

The food was good, really good. Portion size was just right and the taste sensation left us smacking our lips together with pure pleasure. The final stamp of approval was number one son's dessert. He ordered the Rhubarb Custard and Jelly. I know it sounds plain but it was the best part of the whole meal. A big plate of rhubarb doughnuts, custard panna cotta and honeycomb. A large enough portion that satisfied number one son, even after Mrs McEwan and I had dug at it with our spare spoons.

The evening still had legs, so we paid the bill (when I say 'we' I mean 'me') and followed number one son to a cocktail bar of his choosing, *The Revolucion de Cuba*. He brought three identical drinks back to our table, an innocuous looking little yellow number in a Babycham glass with a slice of lime on top. It looked harmless enough - who cares, it was yummy. I didn't find out until the next day it was called a 'Nuclear,' which they 'guaranteed to cause fallout the morning after.' We also tried the 'Brazilian Bramble,' I've no idea what alcohol was in it but it had blackberries the size of my big toe.

The dance floor beckoned and Mrs McEwan and I entertained the throng with our salsa gyrations to music that was as intoxicating as the cocktails. What a brilliant place. What a great night.

Not so great the next morning.

The nuclear did the job it advertised. We made it to breakfast with fifteen minutes to spare and would not have made it at all if we hadn't needed rehydration.

Three pots of coffee later we gathered our stuff and headed home.

Chapter thirteen

LEWIS GRASSIC WHO?

And so to home, gloomy with the thought I might never experience Aberdeen the same way again.

My instinct tells me Aberdeen still has money left in its wallet. Every tenth car is a supercharged gas guzzler. There are expensive restaurants and expensive pubs and very expensive houses, but in the last five years it has changed. When number one son started at university every second or third car was a supercar. There is still oil but less of it and a world glut saw the price drop. In 1980 it was $120 a barrel, it has been as high as $150 a barrel but in 2016 it sat below $40. It became more expensive to recover and less profitable when they do. Oil companies paid off their workers in droves. Aberdeen is now living off its savings.

There is an even greater divide between those with money and those who are surviving. I see nothing to replace the oil industry. Despite its façade, despite the investment in infrastructure, and the abundance of nice cafes I fear that Aberdeen is in decline. On its way to a slow death. Klondike no more. Aberdeen is not so much the 'Granite City' as the 'Grey City.' It is only the optimistic who envision a thriving community thirty years from now. I like Aberdeen and I like the people, so I hope I am wrong.

We were in no rush so I took the scenic coastal route via Stonehaven, Montrose and Arbroath. It had been years since we were last in Stonehaven. The kids were young when we stopped off to visit the open air pool. Going in through the door took us back in time to 1934 - the date the pool opened. To my surprise it was still there.   It is a heated pool, but even in summer we were still cold. No surprise, it's Scotland and within spitting distance of the North Sea.

It is cold up there, okay!

But that wasn't the real problem. The real problem is they fill the pool with salt water. Don't you hate getting a mouthful of salty water? Salt water is something you should only gargle with if you have a throat infection. The salt water caused number two son to come out in a rash. We didn't last long in the pool then, and I had no inclination to try it now. For years the people of Stonehaven campaigned their council to keep the place open, despite it losing money. Who enjoys swimming in cold salty water? Maybe the people who use the static caravan site next door? I bet some of them are masochists.

The static caravan site has about forty, ugly, green and white static caravans sitting in neat rows behind a rickety fence. The residents can stick their heads out of their doors and look at either the Open Air Pool Car Park or other ugly caravans.

Why is it people who have caravans claim to like the outdoors? You never see them sitting outside. I never see them hanging out their knickers on their whirly. They sit inside all day with their doors shut. I'm sorry, but I can't imagine spending two minutes there without going out my mind.

I drove along the sea front, past the *Amusement Arcade*. Two middle-aged ladies exited the open door, but they didn't look amused. The clatter of silver from one of those penny fountains signalled a youth to bend down and pick up his winnings, only to feed them in the top of the machine again. He was unsmiling too. The addictive process reduced his actions to tedium as he emptied his pockets of all his coins. I presumed he would continue until he didn't have a penny left.

Elderly couples packed *Molly's Café Bar* making it look cramped, but they must be doing something right going by the amount of tea and toast on offer. Maybe this was the place that attracted all the caravaners? Maybe they spent their days here, and that was why the only sign of life at the caravan park are the damp pants and socks hanging on a washing line.

In short order I came to a metal fence at the end of the front. I had to do a three-point turn to escape. Beyond the metal fence the stony beach curved inwards in front of the town. It was barren of holidaymakers. On the distant headland I could see the Stonehaven War Memorial: unveiled in 1923 it looks much older, like a columned construction as if it had been built by the Romans. A constant presence on the Stonehaven skyline it sits in ruin looking as fragmentary as the lives of those it commemorates.

We had a brief sojourn to the pretty Stonehaven Harbour. I'd have sat outside and had a coffee at *The Ship Inn* or *The Marine Hotel* but there was nowhere to park. So despite a now full bladder from our morning coffee, we didn't linger and drove on to *Dunnottar Castle*, two miles south of Stonehaven.

Monkeydog likes to stretch his legs, have a pee and sniff lamp posts. Watching him cock his leg on a nearby bush reminded me of the three pots of coffee I had consumed at breakfast. It was time to find a place for me to pee too. We walked out of the car park past the burger van and down the path to the castle. A burger van surviving in a

161

car park shows you how busy the place is. There was a constant trickle of people up and down the path.

Dunnottar Castle is spectacular. The fortress sits perched on a rocky headland, a cliff top on three sides that fall straight down into the ocean. Inaccessible except for one easy to defend path. It is fair to say Dunnottar Castle took my breath away. It is as dramatic a ruin as you will see, beautiful, silent and steeped in history. The best view of the castle is from the edge of the cliff a few hundred yards from the road. It is one of the most impressive views in Scotland.

Monkeydog ran around sniffing his new surroundings with uncontained glee as I stood agog, marvelling at the sight before me. The North Sea washed around the base of the cliffs that stretched up baring its red craggy teeth before flattening out like a birthday cake. The castle tattered and worn as it is, has a noble and defiant air. Still standing after all that has tried to knock it down and weather it away.

It was at Dunnottar Castle that a small garrison held out against the might of Cromwell's army for eight months and saved the Scottish Crown Jewels. They hid *The Honours of Scotland,* (a Crown, a Sceptre and a Sword) there from Oliver Cromwell's invading army in the 17th century. Sir George Ogilvy of Barras, lieutenant-governor of the castle, had the responsibility for their defence. In September 1651 Cromwell's troops appeared at Dunnottar and settled down to a lengthy siege. The garrison of sixty-nine men held out through the winter and spring. It was May before Ogilvy had to surrender when the English brought in heavy guns and for ten days bombarded the castle. Still, Cromwell's men did not find *The Honours of Scotland.*

We Scots are not averse to subterfuge and skullduggery. With eight months to work out a ploy, Ogilvy managed to either smuggle out the Honours of Scotland under the Englishmen's noses or secrete them so well they could not unearth them. The bastards were none too pleased and wreaked revenge by destroying the chapel and imprisoning Ogilvy and his wife. Despite Mrs Ogilvy being tortured to death, neither she nor Ogilvy divulged the whereabouts of the crown, sword or sceptre. The oldest surviving set of crown jewels in the British Isles remained in Scottish hands and The Honours of Scotland are now kept in the Crown Room at Edinburgh Castle.

The first records of habitation at Dunnottar go back to the 4th-century when Saint Ninian, an early missionary of the Pictish people, built a place of worship. Evidence of Picts living there go back to the 3rd century. A team of archaeologists from Aberdeen University discovered a fort nearby, carbon dating showed it to be the oldest Pictish fort ever revealed.

Over the centuries Dunnottar Castle has been the home of Scotland's most powerful families, visited by Mary Queen of Scots and James VI. It has also been used as a prison and the location of a witch burning. In 1715, they convicted the 10th, and last, Earl of Marischal George Keith, of treason for his part in the failed Jacobite rising. The government seized his estates, which included Dunnottar Castle.

More recently filmmakers adapted Dunnottar Castle as the backdrop for Shakespeare's *Hamlet* starring Mel Gibson of *Mad Max* and *Braveheart* fame. It made another appearance in *Victor Frankenstein,* a re-imagined version of Frankenstein starring Daniel Radcliffe and James MacAvoy. Dunnottar Castle is also said to have inspired Disney's animated film *Brave*.

It was the biting wind that first took my attention away from the castle and then the pressing attention of my bladder. Tufted grass covers the headland with footpaths worn away by the multitude of visitors. There are no trees to screen a desperate man looking to respond to the call of nature. Dunnottar Castle has toilets, but I didn't fancy paying the £7 entrance fee. I'm sure it would have been nice to visit, but we weren't stopping for long.

I wandered across the sloping headland looking for a spot to relieve myself out of sight of the various tourists and walkers dotted around. At one point I approached an unmarked cliff edge and had to bellow at Monkeydog to come away as he scampered towards it oblivious to the danger. His attention taken by the smell of a rabbit, no doubt. I sauntered around the headland and turned through 360 degrees, checking for any sightseers who might see me. It was clear. From this lower position, out of sight, I emptied my bladder. Relief at last. I looked up, across the gap to the next headland was a bench and on the bench sat three elderly women wrapped in fawn duffle coats and scarves. They were sitting below the skyline and blended into the background. I tucked my embarrassment out of sight. The three elderly women, in unison, stood up, cheered and clapped. In all my fifty years, it was my first standing ovation. I'm so proud of myself.

We returned to the car, Monkeydog content on the backseat, and headed south.

Before we crossed the bridge into Inverbervie, I saw a tourist information signpost pointing east for the *Grassic Gibbon Centre.* This one had the blue thistle picture, a Scottish Tourist Board Approved Attraction. Theses internationally recognised tourist information signs are made up of white lettering on a brown background. They use ninety-three different symbols to point out the officially recognised 'types' of attractions and facilities across Britain.

"Altogether they encompass a huge variety of interesting places, people to meet, things to do and sights to see, seamlessly incorporating all our history, geography, culture and heritage into a little appreciated and massively underestimated tourist network." (followthebrownsigns.com).

I think they do a good job, I can make a stab at what most of the signs mean; a fish on the end of a hook, a man paddling a canoe, an ice skate, etc. Although there are some difficult ones; a knight praying (apparently a brass rubbing), a horse on a podium in between a fir tree and a deciduous tree (a theme park) and the top of a snail with four various thicknesses of antennae (an English nature reserve). Keep an eye out for them.

I had about twelve seconds to decide. Do I take the detour to the Grassic Gibbon Centre or not?

Lewis Grassic Gibbon was the writer of *Sunset Song* named the best Scottish novel of all time. It tells the story of a young woman growing up in the north-east of Scotland in the early 20th century. *Sunset Song* was the first in the trilogy called *A Scot's Quair,* which included the novels *Cloud Howe* and *Grey Granite,* all three of which have been adapted for television. Sunset Song, the film, was released in 2015 but didn't receive the acclaim afforded to the book. Lewis Grassic Gibbon was a prolific writer, he wrote eighteen novels from 1928 to 1934. He died at aged thirty-three. How many more books he would have contributed to the literary world if he had lived?

A lesser known book of his was *Spartacus* which as the name suggests was an account of the great slave revolt in Ancient Rome. The film *Spartacus* starring Kirk Douglas is based on a book written by Howard Fast and not Gibbon's account. The general belief is Grassic Gibbon's book is a superior version. I don't know - I should add both to my list of reading material. In a departure from his normal writing Gibbon also wrote a science fiction book called *Three Go Back* the story of three men who, after a plane crash, go back 25,000 years in time to the lost island of Atlantis.

I now had six seconds to turn right. Should I visit the Grassic Gibbon Centre or not? I glanced at Mrs McEwan in the passenger seat, she had her eyes closed, maybe not full asleep but dozing. I chose not to disturb her and continued on through Inverbervie. Inverbervie looked a nice little place but I was out the other side and on the road for Montrose before it occurred to me it might have been worth stopping.

Further on we entered Montrose, Mrs McEwan stirred in the passenger seat.

"If I find someplace to stop would you like a coffee?"

"Yes, that would be nice."

"I was going to take a detour to the Grassic Gibbon Centre, but you were dozing."

"The what?"

"Lewis Grassic Gibbon, he has a centre to celebrate his life."

"Who?"

"You know, Sunset Song?"

"What?"

"The book, Sunset Song, Lewis Grassic Gibbon wrote that and Cloud Howe and Grey Granite."

"Never heard of them."

It was maybe just as well I didn't bother stopping. Maybe the Scottish Tourist Board should have a *River City* centre, after the Scottish TV drama series (a soap like Eastenders but in a Scottish accent). You know, a place to celebrate mundane Scottish life where people shout at each other and argue over nothing very much. Mrs McEwan might like to visit a place like that and sit in the corner staring off at some invisible point like it was the actual TV programme. I'd only go if they served coffee and was allowed to take a book.

The way I see it, the world is split into two types of people. There are those who have no idea who Lewis Grassic Gibbon is and there are those, like myself, who have heard of him and one day might actually read one of his books.

Montrose is a bigger place than I'd remembered. It has adventure play parks, open spaces and a wide sandy beach, that extends for four miles to St Cyrus. The town is pretty and possesses many attractions for visitors. It has the fifth and ninth oldest golf clubs in the world. Montrose, has a two mile square lagoon-like basin to its south, a bridge took us over the mud-flats at the mouth of the lagoon and out towards Dundee.

Still looking for a coffee stop, we came to Arbroath and the wrong end of their one way system. I dodged around, found the right end and then couldn't get parked. Arbroath is famous for two things: their delicious Arbroath Smokies ranked in the Great Taste Top 50 Foods in Britain and Arbroath Football Club, which holds the record for the highest number of goals scored in a professional football match. They won 36 - 0 against Aberdeen Bon Accord in the Scottish Cup in 1885. Coincidentally, 1885 was the last time anyone could get parked in Arbroath.

Okay, okay... to save all you Red Lichties* from getting upset there is definitely more to Arbroath than just the smokies and the football team. There is a quaint little harbour and the front has a wide strip of flat grassland before stepping down to the rocky shore. The shore being a place to explore rock pools rather than go for a dip. The path continues a full six miles south to Carnoustie.

*Red Lichties is the nickname for fans of Arbroath F.C. based on a term used to describe someone from Arbroath. It originates from sailors who knew they were coming into Arbroath because it was the only harbour with red lights (licht being a light).

If you like to look at pictures of chips and gravy, listen to a psychic medium's Sunday night message or enter a quiz to win 'your windows cleaned at normal price,' you can join the Facebook group, 'Friends of Red Lichties Online.' (Some posts are just hilarious).

Arbroath Abbey, in the centre of the town, is a fine red stone ruin and steeped in history. Founded by William the Lion in 1178, it became his last resting place. He built the Abbey as a mark of respect to Thomas Becket, the Archbishop of Canturbury who was murdered in 1170. Such was William the Lion's piousness he bequeathed much land and monies to the church.

In 1320, at Arbroath Abbey, thirty-nine Scottish nobles signed the Declaration of Arbroath. A time when

Scotland was still at war with their neighbours south of the border. It is the most famous document in Scottish history, the founding document of the Scottish nation and the basis for the American Declaration of Independence. The most famous line being:-

"As long as but a hundred of us remain alive, never will we on any conditions be brought under English rule. It is in truth not for glory, nor riches, nor honours that we are fighting, but for freedom - for that alone, which no honest man gives up with but life itself."

Perhaps it is that kind of mentality that gives us our fearsome reputation as fighters. Our tribal nature is the glue that binds us and gives us strength. There is a saying parents in Germany use to scare their children that translates to, 'wait until the Scotsman comes to get you.'

Somewhere between Arbroath and Dundee we stopped at a Dobbies Garden Centre, lured by the thought of coffee and cake.

Did you know it was an ex-cop who started the business (PC Dobbie, I presume); he was a keen gardener growing plants in his back garden. Someone asked if they could buy one and so he potted them and sold them to friends and neighbours. People got to know about his small enterprise and the business just grew and grew.

I like Dobbies Garden Centres. This one was very similar to the one I go to near Stirling; it had the same inefficient customer service system. We had the usual long queue at the restaurant, and it wasn't even lunchtime. I stood waiting, eyeing the strawberry tart I'd chosen and imagining how messy it would be to eat.

We were being served by a large fat man, well beyond overweight. He had a brutal expression on his face as if someone had just wiped a snotter on his shoulder and he wasn't sure which one of us it was. He had a hairnet pulled tight over his short black hair, which was odd because the other female staff behind the counter all had long hair but no hairnets. I wondered if he had alopecia or dandruff something. The net pulled at his forehead giving him a look of surprised anger as if that 'wiping a snotter on his shoulder' thing had just happened. He wouldn't have looked out of place in an American all-you-can-eat buffet for executioners.

I watched him with the interest one has in watching someone who is not enjoying themselves - when you are not enjoying yourself. I hate queues, but there I was standing in a queue feeling irritated by the inefficiency of a Dobbies Garden Centre café once again. I surmised the obese server was not enjoying himself because they were busy and he couldn't find an excuse to go back to the kitchen and eat all the leftovers. The old couple in front of me ordered two coffees, Mr Obese grabbed two mugs from the stack. He grabbed them with his great big paws, thumbs on the outside and fingers right inside. Yuck!. I vowed if he did that with my mugs I would ask him to change them.

Then it came my turn.

"What do you want?" he said without trace of a smile.

"A cappuccino and a latte, please."

He waddled over to the stack of mugs. His right hand picked up one mug from the base but with his left hand he dipped his fingers right into the mug to grip it and carry it to the coffee machine. I asked him to change it and explained why. He apologised but I must have made him angry because three minutes after we sat down I saw him knock over a mug and saucer causing them to smash on the floor. I sipped at my coffee, irritated because it wasn't as piping hot as I like it and for having to put my head above the parapet to challenge Mr Obese and his poor hygiene standards.

I don't normally say anything to staff about poor service, especially staff who look like they might choke me to death and bury me in the garden. I vote with my feet. I walk out and never go back. Restaurants don't survive that kind of vote.

Sometimes I speak up when I shouldn't. It can come across as offensive or insulting. Sometimes I should've spoken up but didn't. I don't want to give a bad impression or instead, I wait and worry. A friend of mine once pointed out that we often feel guilty when we stand up to people. Why should we feel at fault when we are doing what is right? Our mind and conscience is a funny thing.

What I should have done is supported the elderly couple in front of me. I shouldn't have waited until it affected me, I should have put my neck above the parapet for the old couple and asked Mr Obese to change their mugs.

I've made mistakes.

Maybe you have too? Most people who get a tattoo come to regret their decision, it might not be for many years but while our opinions change, that ink stain stays the same. Some regret it the moment they walk out of the tattoo parlour. Regret requires us to imagine how our life will be if we did or didn't do something in our past. Would we be happier if it had or hadn't happened? It can be painful thinking about what we could have done that would have led to a better outcome.

If we make the wrong choices it makes us unhappy, we enter a phase of denial, then bewilderment; How could I have done that? What was I thinking? Then we move on to kick ourselves, a phase of self-punishment. In the end, we have a wake-up call. We learn from our mistakes. A good thing comes of it.

However, it is possible to learn from the mistakes of others. An important lesson can filter through to the brain without having to make a permanent ink mark on your body. I later learned the Grassic Gibbon Centre has a café serving good coffee and home baking and I regret not stopping there.

So if you ever see that sign post, turn off and go drop in.

Chapter fourteen

MULL IT OVER

The best 25th wedding anniversary I ever went on was to Mull.

Mrs McEwan and I took the old Jag and gunned our way through the beautiful Trossachs, Strathyre, and Crianlarich, before turning left past the famous Green Welly Shop in Tyndrum. The A85 from Tyndrum to Oban is spectacular as it meanders its way between the majestic hills. The waters of Lochan na Bi open out and stay with you for nearly a mile, then the route follows the River Lochy all the way to Inverlochy (blink and you'll miss it).

We continued to Oban through some of the most beautiful countryside. Even the drizzly rain didn't detract from the stunning hills, lochs and glens. Although, I hoped we might get drier weather over the weekend.

A mile outside Oban, the road drops steeply into the town. The pace slowed to a dawdle and then a dead stop as we joined a line of traffic. We crawled along stop starting and stopped again. An old lady with a walking frame zoomed by us on the pavement. I glimpsed the Sound of Kerrera and Mull in the distance. My plan was to stop in Oban for a leisurely coffee before catching our ferry, but we inched along so slowly I worried we might not make it in time for the boat. I glanced at my watch. What the hell was the problem?

We edged along on the outskirts of town; it was tortuously slow. What was holding us up? I checked my watch with increasing frequency. A pickup truck came up the hill and I let it cross in front of us as it turned down a side street to our left. In one of those 'get this wrong and I'll bring it up at every opportunity' moments, I followed the pickup truck to see if the road would take me an alternative route into town. I don't know Oban all that well, but it turned out to be a fortuitous decision. I descended through a housing scheme, past a primary school and came out at the end of the shops. That impulsive move cut at least forty minutes off the wait. We arrived in the town centre and saw the *Oban Fish & Chip* takeaway restaurant in the main street had been on fire. The fire services doused the last remaining embers. A lone police officer directed traffic. Alternately, he let the cars past on the remaining single lane, this explained the delay. If there is a real hold-up on the roads there is always some poor cop directing traffic.

The shortcut paid off, we parked up outside the ferry terminal in good time and went in search of a coffee. We decided on *The Coffee Shop* on the ground floor of the *Perle Oban Hotel*. That was a mistake. The staff hadn't a clue. It was a model of inefficiency and incompetence. I stood at the bar waiting to give my order for several minutes while four of the bar staff scratched their heads trying to decipher who had ordered what. It looked like a scene from *Good Will Hunting*, the one where the class stare at the complicated figures and equations on the blackboard in puzzlement. As I stood there another waiter approached my wife, as she sat alone at our table, and asked if she had ordered the soup.

"No, We have just arrived. My husband is up there at the bar trying to order some coffee."

Eventually, I got their attention and gave our order, a Latte, a Cappuccino and two biscuits. I sat down and waited. It was a nice enough place, recently refurbished by the look of it and had comfortable seating. Mrs McEwan has a background in catering. She has managed some large

174

restaurants, it amused her how totally useless the staff were. How long does it take four people to make two cups of coffee and put a couple of biscuits on a plate? We both made light of it, not wanting to spoil the weekend before it even started. However, after being asked three times by a waiter if we had ordered burgers, I made my way back to the bar and informed them that if we didn't get our coffee and biscuits soon we would have to leave because we didn't want to miss our ferry.

"I'm sorry, we have only just opened and we are still trying to get our heads around how everything works."

"That explains everything," not wanting to make a fuss, "so this is your first day?"

"No," he replied, "we opened three weeks ago."

Oops!

As politely as I could, I asked if they could wouldn't mind removing their heads from their backsides and pour us a coffee, "if you could do that, that would be nice."

I returned to our table and Mrs McEwan suppressed a giggle, amused they had been open for three weeks and not three minutes. Our coffees arrived and I have to admit, they tasted delicious. So good, in fact, I reversed my decision never to cross their doorstep ever again. I will absolutely return for a coffee whenever I am back in Oban. Although, I might wait a few months first - just to make sure they have their act together.

Now I am going to tell you about the best place you could possibly buy seafood.

It's on the pier at Oban. Just behind the ferry terminal is a seafood shack. It is just a little shack with a few tables and benches outside and a sign above that says 'Local

Shellfish.' The choice and quality on offer is impressive; lobsters, crabs, mussels, oysters, and langoustines that looked so fresh I swear their eyes followed me as I edged up the queue. In the end, I opted for a double salmon sandwich and a double prawn sandwich, both on fresh brown bread. Something for us to munch on the ferry to Mull. The shack was busy but there were plenty of staff buzzing around to get the job done. Not only that, the staff were the friendliest people, I don't think I have seen any shop where staff smile so much, they unmistakably enjoyed what they were doing.

On the ferry we made our way to the observation deck and admired the view. Dominating the town of Oban, on Battery Hill, is McCaig's Tower (known locally as McCaig's Folly), a monstrous but somehow engaging granite rotunda resembling Rome's Colosseum. Commissioned in 1897 by John McCaig, an eccentric banker, to commemorate his family and provide work for the locals in winter. Today it is an empty shell, which is more than 650 feet in circumference. His plans to incorporate a museum and art gallery with a central tower was brought to an end with his death in 1902. Instead there is a nice garden in which to contemplate life, the universe and everything. From experience, the walk to the top and the spectacular views it offers of Oban Bay are as good a hangover cure as any.

Mrs McEwan and I found a table and sat next to a bubbly lady who was working on a laptop. By this time I was salivating over the sandwiches. Even through the cling film wrapper I could see they were thick with salmon and bursting with prawns. I was eager to get tucked in. However, we got talking to Denise, our table companion, and it seemed a bit rude to start munching food. So instead of sating my hunger I played my travel game.

176

One of the best things about travelling is meeting other people. It always delights me to find out just how boring a life others lead. It makes my life seem not so bad. Then, once in a while, you get to meet someone who is interesting. When you do, journeys pass in the flutter of a butterfly's wings.

There is a theory that every person on the planet is connected to every other person in the world through a chain of acquaintances that has no more than five intermediaries. It is commonly known as 'six degrees of separation.' The theory was first proposed in 1929 by Frigyes Karinthy, a Hungarian writer. Mathematicians have tried to prove the theory by coming up with equations in explanation, too complicated for me to understand. It appears they didn't understand them either because they were unable to solve the problem to their satisfaction. The theory wasn't proved until 1967 when an American sociologist, Stanley Milgram, devised an ingenious test. Milgram randomly selected people to send packages to an arbitrary stranger located in another part of the country. The senders were given the name, occupation and general location of the person, that was all. Their instructions were to send the package to a person they knew on a first-name basis, who was most likely, to know the stranger personally. That person would do the same, and so on until the package was delivered to the stranger. The expectation was that it would take hundreds of intermediaries before the package ended up at the correct recipient. However, he discovered it only took six people, on average, for the package to be delivered successfully.

So this is the game I play. When I meet a stranger or fellow traveller, I look for the six degrees of separation. Denise, as it turned out, went to school in a small village a couple of miles from me. We mentioned several names and discovered a mutual friend. There we were, strangers on a ferry, with only one degree of separation.

I was interested to learn Denise had a background in Human Resources. One day she upped sticks and moved to Tobermory to bring up her family. With her knowledge and connections she and her friend started a recruitment business.

How on earth do you run a recruitment business from the back of beyond?

Well, it appears you can. There might be difficulties, but they can be overcome. Denise is the Managing Director of *Cazden* a thriving business that has clients all over the UK. It was intriguing to hear how she runs a busy business and still reaps the benefits of a chilled out life on Mull.

"Aren't you going to eat your sandwiches?" she asked.

It was all the encouragement I needed. And they were delicious, sumptuous even. I can honestly say I have never had a salmon sandwich like it. It was stuffed with pinky goodness. The prawn sandwich was just as good. The sauce was perfect and even when it dribbled down my chin I couldn't just wipe it away. I scooped it up on my finger and deposited it back in my mouth. I made a mental note to stop at the shack on the road home and treat ourselves to more. I can assure you these were no ordinary sandwiches, they are a must try - if you are anywhere near Oban.

Another useful thing about talking to locals is that you can ask them where are the best places to go. Denise recommended the *Glengorm Coffee Shop* near Glengorm Castle.

"My friend runs the place and you won't get a better bit of cake," she advised.

Stepping off the ferry on to Mull felt like I was stepping back in time. Except I didn't step off the ferry, I drove off behind an ancient Volkswagen camper van, it had a dateless number plate. The paintwork was so sun bleached it almost had no colour at all. Disgorged from the mouth of our Caledonian MacBrayne ferry I waited behind a row of cars to join the road.

A left turn would take me on to the single track road to Fionnphort where the ferry makes the short crossing to the small island of Iona and what feels like 1759. It was a journey I made as a teenager. I camped for a week with my youth fellowship group in the grounds of Iona Abbey. It is a very spiritual place. There has been a monastery there since St Columba founded it in the year 563. My lasting memory of the trip was canoodling with a girl in the Bishop's quarter on the top floor of the Abbey. Now there is a time I wouldn't mind going back to.

Instead, I turned right into what feels like a more modern 1957 and drove the short distance to our hotel on the north side of Craignure. When a ferry arrives in port and everyone drives off onto a small island and there is only one road, it can get busy. We got stuck in a line of traffic, going only as fast as the slowest driver ahead. Queuing theory dictates that the further down the line you are, the slower you go. One person touches their brake slightly at the head of the queue and this is multiplied as it passes down the line. Inevitably, ten cars back, we came to a dead stop. I, like every other driver, was in a hurry to get to our hotel to avoid a long wait in reception. We made it to the *Isle of Mull Hotel*

& *Spa* behind three cars. About a dozen more followed us into the car park. I recognised the need - the need for speed. I abandoned the car as near to the entrance as I could. In a flash I alighted and removed our luggage from the boot. Unfortunately, Mrs McEwan was still in the passenger seat, staring at the visor mirror and putting on her lipstick. I weighed up my options. Here we were on our 25th anniversary trip and I didn't want to spoil it by falling out with her, nor did I want stuck in reception for the duration of our stay. We were only there for the weekend. As politely as I could, I asked Mrs McEwan to get a move on.

"You look fine. C'mon, let's get in before we get stuck in a crowd at reception."

"Don't be such a grump," she berated.

A further seven cars entered the car park, came to a halt and people emerged and grabbed their luggage in a hurry to get ahead in the queue.

"Get your erse oot the car noo!" I said encouragingly and thumbed in the direction of the mobbed car park.

We did the short walk into the hotel at double time, overtaking an elderly couple to get to the door first. Admittedly, I had to kick one of their trolley suitcases out of their hands to slow them down, but the tactic worked. As overtaking manoeuvres go, eat your heart out Lewis Hamilton.

Despite being only the third couple in the queue, we still had an interminably long wait. An old wooden bureau, next to the reception desk, displayed all the obligatory tourist information brochures. I looked in the two drawers and saw we had the option to play chess, draughts or dominoes. There were no packs of cards. Once I had read all the tourist leaflets (twice) we eventually got checked in and a porter showed us to our room.

On the sideboard was a bucket of ice and a bottle of champagne I'd ordered when booking. A nice surprise for Mrs McEwan but a shock for me when I pulled it out and saw it wasn't champagne but prosecco. I don't mind drinking prosecco, so I didn't make a fuss, especially as they had also placed a plate of chocolate covered strawberries beside it. That was a nice touch. I made a mental note to check the bill at the end of our stay to make sure I was paying for overpriced prosecco rather than overpriced champagne.

There was an additional problem. As much as they had been good enough to ensure a cold bottle of fizz was waiting and they had gone out of their way to give the silver anniversary couple a free plate of chocolate covered strawberries, there was still a hitch - the room was a twin, two single beds. On the off chance there was a hiatus between the hot flushes, the stars aligning and Mrs McEwan being in the mood, (similar chance of winning the lottery) I thought it my marital duty to ask that we be relocated to a double room.

Well you never know. If you're not in it - you can't win it!

I had to go back to the reception and wait in another interminably long queue to speak to the receptionist and get it sorted. The double room we were moved to was about a three-mile walk along corridors, up stairs, along another corridor, down other stairs and right at the end of the building. It didn't matter. We were in a good mood and the view from the room was stunning.

The Isle of Mull Hotel & Spa is part of a chain of Crerar Hotels. I have stayed at several of their hotels. On the whole they are clean, friendly and excellent value. The Isle of Mull Hotel & Spa sits overlooking Craignure Bay on the Sound of Mull with views back across to Oban and the deep dark waters of Loch Linnhe. It is easy to see why people come to Mull and immediately fall in love with it. I took a panoramic picture and posted it on Google Maps. Occasionally, I get an email from the nice people at Google informing me that so many thousands of people have viewed it, good to know.

With the chocolate strawberries in our bellies, washed down by two glasses of prosecco, we took a walk to the shore.

No lottery win that afternoon.

The garden of the hotel battles with the local flora and fauna for space. The local flora being bracken and the local fauna being midges. We followed a path through the ferns down to the water and into a cloud of the little blighters. Some people don't like bats but the common pipistrelle bat is an adorable little creature. A tiny little thing that could curl up and fall asleep on your pinkie. I love it most for its ability to consume the little highland hooligans. Each tiny pipistrelle can consume as much as 3,000 midges every single night.

Just as we were about to get eaten alive, a breeze whipped up and kept the midges at bay. A path along the shore took as back out at Craignure and I popped into the local Spar shop to buy a pack of cards to donate to the hotel (once we got fed up with playing with them). The walk there and back sufficed to work up a thirst, and we made our way to the bar for an aperitif.

The lounge and the dining room at The Isle of Mull Hotel & Spa both have stunning views over the water. In the lounge, we watched as a schooner moored in the bay and a small boat ferried rich people to the shore. The sun headed towards the horizon. It looked so tranquil; we sat quiet and happy until it was time to eat.

At the restaurant, we waited behind a handsome couple to be seated. I saw a large table at the far side with reserved plaques. The man, a tall and distinguished looking fellow, looked upside down at the reservations book and all excited turned and whispered to his wife.

She let out a squeal, "Really?"

"Yes, they must be the ones who have booked big table."

They turned to us, all smiles, he said, "you will never believe who we are eating with in our restaurant tonight."

"Who?"

"Metallica, it's in the reservations book, there is a big block booking with 'Metallica' written across it."

"Metallica?"

"Yes, Metallica. They are a great American rock band."

I put two and two together. "I saw a schooner arrive in the bay and a lot of rich people getting off. It must be the band."

"Yes," he smiled, "and they must be coming here to dine, I need to phone my nephew, he loves them."

He whipped out his mobile phone and dialled a number. Within seconds he was relating the story and promising to get autographs for the lad on the other end of the phone.

A group of elderly Italians shuffled into the restaurant behind us. I had one of those curious moments when something didn't feel quite right. I looked at the reservations book and realised the tall handsome man in front of me had read it wrong. I tapped him on the shoulder and pointed at the reservations book and with my other hand I turned to book to face the right way up. The block booking was in fact for 'Mac Italia' and it was the elderly Italians behind us who had the table reserved.

I ordered champagne and we sat by the window in the restaurant, dining on our perfectly cooked steaks. The champagne tasted like the drink of the gods, fizzing over my tongue like heavy rain falling on a cracked-mud riverbed. The combination of alcohol, a full belly and the dramatic sunset bathed us in a gentle calm. I was mellowed by the intoxicating wine and in awe of the beauty of the Sound of Mull. If there were a time to have the apocalypse, it would be then.

The next day, after a light breakfast of cereal, buttered toast, sausage, bacon, eggs, tattie scone, haggis, black pudding, more buttered toast, mushrooms, tomatoes, ham, cheese, smoked salmon, mixed fruit covered in yoghurt and three cups of coffee to wash down the last of the buttered toast and jam, we headed out to explore Mull.

Mull could just about fit inside the M25 circular around London, which is only slightly bigger than New York City (NYC). So it would take a lot longer to explore than the one day we had. There are over ten million people living inside the M25 and the same in NYC. Not so many on Mull. The population swells during the tourist season, but there are less than three thousand permanent residents.

Our first port of call was to Duart Castle which sits proud on the craggy cliffs to the South of Craignure. Originally the family home of the Clan MacLean, at various stages in its history, it has been invaded, attacked and demolished by rival clans, Scottish kings and troops fighting on behalf of Oliver Cromwell. Duart Castle was brought back from ruin in 1911. The castle sits on a headland accessed via a two mile long single-track road. It's daunting to squeeze into a passing place as a big bus approaches and slips by with inches to spare. From the car park to the castle is a large well manicured lawn. The headland looks out across the crescent-shaped bay that cradles Craignure and from there you can watch the Caledonian MacBrayne ferry creep behind the castle into port.

We noticed a sign for the *Millennium Wood* and entered via a gate to explore. It is a short walk in a circular route through a thicket. Little placards identify the fauna and detail information about the trees and scrubs. I didn't know, for example, that the Scots pine tree is Scotland's only native conifer (apart from the juniper, which is more of a bush than a tree). Ah! the juniper - little wonder that Scotland has a thriving gin industry.

Following our walk in the woods, we made our way to the entrance of the castle and spoke to an enthusiastic lady in a small wooden shed who attended the ticket office. She had a book on her lap that was something to do with the history of the Clan MacLean. I asked one question, and that was enough for her to spout forth, excited about all things MacLean. She was very knowledgeable and her enthusiasm was infectious. We purchased tickets and went on a tour of the castle.

We entered the main keep at Duart, built by Lachlan Lubanach in the 1390s. Lachlan is a great Scottish name - although you have to be born and bred in Scotland to pronounce it correctly. We meandered our way through the kitchen quarters along the bare corridors and shuddered at the cold dark dungeon imagining the horror of being incarcerated in such a frightening place. Climbing the stairs to the upper level it opened out into a hallway dotted with various interesting artefacts and paraphernalia collected over the years. What stunned me most was the view. The window stretched the full length of the hallway with a ledge underneath. I sat, slightly twisted, to look out to sea. It was no ordinary view. Looking straight up Loch Linnhe the white of a lighthouse stood out in the black water separated at the southern end of the low-lying Isle of Lismore. The Isle of Lismore sits directly over the Great Glen Fault that divides Scotland into two parts. Considered one of the most fertile islands of Scotland because the island is entirely composed of Dalradian limestone. It is likely, due to its fertile soil, that it once supported a much larger population. Today there are only two-hundred residents on the ten-mile long one-mile wide island. During the 1800s that figure would have been nearly fifteen-hundred. In the 1970s the island population dropped to a low of one hundred, so perhaps people are being attracted back.

It was such a clear day we could see Glencoe and Ben Nevis in the distance, both making for an imposing setting. There may not have been much to do for the MacLean clan ancestors in Duart Castle on a wet and blustery day in winter, other than wrap up warm and light a fire. However, on a clear summers day the view alone is worth all the efforts of the current incumbent to restore and maintain it.

There was information posted on the wall detailing how the MacLean and Campbell clans came to have a deep ingrained animosity towards each other. The 11th chief of the MacLeans, Lachlan Cattanach, or 'Lachlan the Hairy' as people knew him, married Elizabeth Campbell. Elizabeth could not conceive him a child, (I wonder if this was anything to do with her husband's hirsute body putting her off) so he plotted to murder her. He marooned her on rocks on the Sound of Mull, leaving her to her fate as the tides rose. Left to drown in what would look like an accident. Fortunately for Elizabeth, some local fishermen spotted her and carted her off the rocks to the safety of her father, the Earl of Argyll. Lachlan had already been to visit the family and offer his condolences. The Earl of Argyll invited Lachlan back the next day for dinner only for Lachlan to find his drowned wife seated at the table. And there the rivalry began. I'm not sure how Lachlan got out of the Campbell home unscathed, but he did get what was coming. After marrying twice more and having three children, Lachlan was murdered by a Campbell.

The things people will do for kids!

I wandered through the rest of the castle. There were sufficient antiques and items of interest in the great hall to grab my attention. At the far end, silver goblets, cups, candleware and a tureen were lit up in a glass case. Interesting as they were, I was taken with the fact that the display was set up on an old slate snooker table and thought it a shame it may never again be used for its original purpose.

The team are doing a wonderful job in restoring it. The castle, I am informed, receives about 25,000 visitors a year and this must go some way to help with the not inconsiderable costs of upkeep. The castle is still being invaded and attacked, not by rival clans or the English, but by the relentless bad weather. For a good part of the year it can be very windy and wet.

The clan name of MacLean can be spelled in at least fifteen different ways. As the ancestral home, Duart Castle should interest all the various strands of descendants from all over the world. There is a lady in Florida who sends donations from her supermarket wages. I sincerely hope my entrance fee and other such donations will be enough to keep it from crumbling to the ground.

We descended the stairs at the far side of the castle and made our way past the current incumbents lodgings. Sir Lachlan Hector Charles MacLean, the 28th chief of the Scottish clan and 12th Baronet of Morvern live in rooms on the ground floor, not accessible to the public, but through the small window panes I could see it was slightly snugger than the rest of the castle, albeit cluttered and lived in.

Emerging from our trip back in time I thanked the lady at the entrance booth and she was delighted that we had enjoyed our visit. We popped our head into the café and gift shop for a look around, bought a book then headed back to the car to take ourselves to Glengorm Castle and the coffee shop Denise had recommended.

To get there I had to drive back down the single track road for two miles and join the main road again. Back down to Craignure the road widens to a two-lane highway, and I toddled along admiring the scenery passing places like the port of *Fishnish,* which is literally just a house, two sheds and some chickens. Then *Glenforsa*, which has Mull's only airfield. I drove in to have a look.

The airfield is operated by the *Glenforsa Hotel*, a Norwegian wooden log construction. The airfield sits between the hotel and the Sound of Mull, and is merely a well maintained strip of lawn that looks about the length of grass between the stumps on a cricket pitch (if you are flying in, it is much longer really). Patrons who bring their own aircraft have ample parking facilities next to the hotel. I pictured that a hotel with its own airfield might be a large posh affair, instead it was small, delightful and friendly. How magic it must be to jump in your own aeroplane zoom across the water and arrive at Glenforsa ten minutes later for afternoon tea. People must do it because there were half a dozen tiny aircraft scattered about the lawn. The Glenforsa Hotel is a family-owned hotel with eleven reasonably priced en-suite rooms. The menu looked pretty delicious too, but we turned about and headed on.

A little further on we passed through the small hamlet of *Salen* and the road narrowed once again to a single track with passing places. It didn't matter. Pulling in to the side of the road to allow oncoming traffic to pass and being allowed to admire the views for a second or two longer was divine. Passing oncoming traffic was always a good-mannered experience. Every driver pulled in to let cars past at the first opportunity. Even local tradesmen didn't seem to be in any hurry. It must be almost perfect living and working in a place where you never tire of the views.

In due course, we arrived in Tobermory, the outskirts are dotted with excavations for new builds and impressive new homes. A short drop down to the bay and we were met with the iconic view of the colourful buildings that overlook the water.

My Dad used to say he was the worst singer in Scotland. That was until he married my Mum - then he became the second worst singer in Scotland. In the fullness of time my older brother came along, they nurtured him and he grew from a tiny baby into a toddler, he began walking and then talking. The day came when he too tried to sing

189

and on that day my Dad realised he had become the third worst singer in Scotland. All four of his children (including myself), inherited his 'tone-deaf' gene. So with a wife and four children my Dad confidently pronounced he is now only the sixth worst singer in Scotland. I come from a long line of musically inept and tone-deaf forefathers. There is a reason for telling you this.

As soon as we arrived at the Main Street overlooking the bay and saw all those vibrant multi-coloured buildings we were reminded of a children's TV programme. Mrs McEwan and I sparked up a rendition of the theme tune to *Balamory.*

Balamory, Balamory
What's the story in Balamory
Wouldn't you like to know?

But we only got a three lines in when I forgot the words and by then my wife had become disenchanted with my tuneless crooning anyway (it doesn't take long).

The children's TV programme was about a small fictional island community called *Balamory* in Scotland and was mostly filmed in Tobermory. The BBC produced it for three years between 2002 and 2005, and in that time they knocked out 254 episodes. Number three son was aged two when it started so I got to enjoy every single one of those programmes. You would think I would remember more than two lines of the theme song. It isn't until you visit Tobermory you realise *Balamory* wasn't a fictional children's TV programme but a documentary with the name changed.

Tobermory is about as perfect a little place to visit as you can imagine. Entering the Main Street I passed the Tobermory Distillery on the right. If I had more time, I would have liked to have taken a tour, next time maybe. I know they do various aged malts that I'd like to try, including a 42-year-old Ledaig Dusgadh (meaning 'awakening' in Scots Gaelic) looking at the bottle and the stunning chestnut coloured contents is about as near as I will ever get to it.

At £3,500 a bottle I'd rather buy a car.

I worked out, in my head, that I could also buy 140 pretty decent other Scotch malts or 600 bottles of presentable wine or 1200 pints of Samuel Smiths Organic Lager. So I'd need to be as well off as Warren Buffett to feel justified in buying a bottle the Ledaig.

I used to work with a guy, let's call him Uncle Sylvester, who only ever ate burger and chips. If the restaurant didn't serve burger and chips, then he wouldn't go in. I asked him one day why he always chose burger and chips.

"I like burger and chips," he said.

"But you might like something else on the menu."

"What if I don't like it?"

"You might find you do, that's the point."

"Yeah, but what if I don't like it? Then I will have just wasted my money."

"Life shouldn't be boring, experiencing new things can be a delight. Variety is the spice of life. You will never know what you are missing if you don't try something new."

Uncle Sylvester looked at me and replied, "I know what I'll miss, I'll miss burger and chips."

I told Uncle Sylvester the story about my Mum and Dad. They were both retired and once a week they took a trip into town and had lunch. Their preferred restaurant served Indian cuisine and a small choice of western food. They ignored all the delicious Indian food on offer and opted for soup for starters then fish and chips, which the Indian restaurant provided at a very reasonable price. Then one day, I joined them.

"What's that you have ordered?" my Dad asked as my starter arrived.

"Vegetable pakora," I replied, "would you like a taste?"

From his first bite he was smitten. He loved it. He couldn't believe what he had been missing. My Mum tried a bite, and her eyes lit up at the taste sensation. From then on, whenever they went to the Indian restaurant they ordered vegetable pakora, then fish and chips. Some months later I took them out to lunch again. They both ordered vegetable pakora and fish and chips. I ordered chicken pakora as a starter and chicken tikka as a main meal. No sooner was it placed in front of me they had their forks in their hands and stabbed at my plate to try it. The chicken pakora blew them away.

"That chicken pakora is even better than the vegetable pakora," they said in unison.

"Wait until you try the chicken tikka," I said. And they did. They tucked into my meal as if it was the first time they had eaten in weeks.

Now my Mum and Dad order chicken pakoras and chicken tikka meals when they go out and they love it.

Uncle Sylvester looked at me suspiciously, "Do they try any other dishes from the Indian?"

"Oh, I think they occasionally do."

"Did they like them all?"

"Well, I don't think they were keen on the lamb vindaloo."

"Exactly, that's why I always have a burger and chips. I know I like burger and chips."

It was this conversation that came to mind when I passed the *Tobermory Distillery*. I thought about the £3,500 bottle of Ladaig Dusgadh and whether I would like it. It was a lot of money to spend even if I loved it, but what if I didn't? Suddenly, I knew where Uncle Sylvester was coming from. Stick with burger and chips if you like, but if you get the chance to grab a bite of chicken pakora from someone else's plate or a sip of Ladaig Dusgadh from someone else's bottle, then do that.

Tobermory isn't all that big a place. It has a population of about one thousand and all the interesting things to see are concentrated around the harbour. Behind the Main Street is a steep hill the locals have a climb to get to their quaint little cottages. A climb that is worth every step. From their elevated viewpoints they have spectacular views to watch the world sail by.

The Main Street is a charming place to poke your nose in. What Las Vegas does with neon-soaked flashing lights along its strip, Tobermory does with six tins of multi-coloured gloss paint. There are several unusual shops and cafes that reflect the entrepreneurial spirit of the business owners. It is such a delight to walk into these independent retailers and try on hats and jackets that you just can't buy anywhere else. There are many items of interest to pass the time. Before I knew it I had a bag stuffed with trinkets and baubles. Next to the Distillery was a shop that sold excellent soft jumpers, hard-wearing trousers and walking boots. All the things people ensure they have on a trip to Mull before they get there but wish they had waited and bought there because the quality is second to none.

At the end of the pier is the *Sealife Visitor Centre* that houses the Mull Aquarium. It was handy to pop into for a pee and, again, had we had more time I would have definitely had a saunter through the Aquarium. Instead we wandered to the end of the pier and took many photographs of the colourful houses around the harbour. Pictures with old anchors in the foreground and a washed out blue rowing boat. It was a calm sunny day, and the results were pleasing to the eye. Dozens of photographs that whenever I look at them make me want to go back.

Along the Main Street there were a couple of cafes that tempted us. One also sold a plethora of interesting and unusual little trinkets. It smelled so delicious we would have stopped off for coffee and cake but we weren't the only ones who thought it irresistible, all tables being taken. The *Isle of Mull Soap Co* was next to an antique store and a bar and lounge. Then *Mull Pottery Shop.* Before long we reached the end of the street and had to turn about and head back to the car. I also noticed an advert for entertainment. For one night only, at a nearby theatre in the form of Jeremy Hardy, an erudite English comedian.

Tobermory would make a nice relaxing base to stay and explore the Island. I could happily guddle about inTobermory for a week or two .

With the delicious smells whetting our appetite we carried on to our destination. Getting to the coffee shop at Glengorm Castle meant taking an even narrower and winding single track road for four miles across the north side of the island. There is a steep climb up through Tobermory and we passed lovely cottages whose doorsteps were inches from the road. I noticed some had small postage stamp gardens over a wall on the opposite side of the road from their cottages. Little well presented patches of grass, with herbaceous borders, a single table and bench. Ideal spots overlooking the bay and the yachts bobbing about in the water - ideal at least if there was a sufficient breeze to keep the midges away.

One garden had a small garden hut, with a triangular felt roof. Windows at the front and a wooden slatted back. Their own two person viewpoint, all private and cosy. I could picture myself in there with a glass of wine and a good book, popping my head up now and then to admire the scenery. Safe from the world and the dreaded midge.

If you haven't got a sufficient breeze or a small garden hut, then my advice is to do what the Royal Marines do. Treacherous terrain. Sweaty jungles. Stinging cold. Hostile territory. Midges. None of those stand in their way. It can't, because what makes them elite is getting the job done. So what do they do for midges? - They moisturise.

Avon's Skin So Soft dry oil spray smells better and is cheaper than most mosquito repellents and is surprisingly effective at deterring the little blighters. You will struggle to find a marine who doesn't have improved skin tone and texture.

"There is nothing effeminate about it," said a burly commando, "we use it because it is good kit. It works."

Fairway bunkers. Torrential rain. Crosswinds. Fresh air shots. Midges. None of those stand in the way of a good golfer. Not with a Skin So Soft spray in their golf bag.

We drove along a rough road, over cattle grids and through craggy terrain. Snaked in between some forestry commission land full of fir trees and man-made ditches at the side of the road. We came across a white bungalow, the grounds of which were enclosed in a neat dry stone dyke. I wondered what the people who lived there did all day. Have their porridge in the morning and play the bagpipes? Or just scowl at passing traffic all day long? I got the impression it was the latter.

Then the road hugged the side of a rough crag to our left and twisted us around until the land opened up in front of us and we could see the Atlantic stretching out to the horizon. In the distance, Glengorm Castle perched on the headland. What a view - jings it wis braw - I drew into the side of the road and stopped to admire it. At that very moment a Hen Harrier swooped down and perched on a wooden fence post not ten feet from the car. The weight of it caused the rickety wooden stave to bend at an angle so that the Hen Harrier was eye level with me. It was a beauty. I couldn't take my eyes from it. The Hen Harrier balanced itself then turned and stared right back at me. It's pitch black pupils, set in yellow, eyed me with what I took to be disdain. It was the most majestic looking bird of prey I have ever seen. Then, after about ten seconds, it stretched out its wings. It had attractive brown and white markings and in two flaps of its wings it was away. Soaring down the valley searching out its next meal, no doubt. Suddenly, it swooped to the ground, then did an aerobatic sky dance as it failed to locate its prey. It was an awesome spectacle. Mrs McEwan and I were speechless. We sat in appreciable silence, happy to have taken this potholed route.

I hadn't known it was a Hen Harrier. I had to ask the font of all knowledge. Google informed me that the brown markings indicated it was a female. Male Hen Harriers have a white plumage and black tipped wings like a Russian jet fighter. Of all the birds of prey in the UK the Hen Harrier is the most intensively persecuted. It effects the number of

196

grouse available to shoot and that conflict threatens its survival. The Hen Harrier is on the brink, especially in England where there are only a handful of breeding pairs left. To see this bird on Mull was a truly magnificent sight. I hope they will still be there to thrill my children with their dance through the skies in the years to come.

The bird disappeared from sight and after a few minutes reflection I started up the car and continued on to the white gated entrance to Glengorm Castle. There the road split into two and a signpost directed us to the right for the coffee shop. Despite it being in such an out of the way location, the car park - if you could call it that - was full. Ten cars squeezed onto a patch of slippery ground and ten more were tight to a wall on the other side of the road. I breathed in enough to squeeze the car into a spot that didn't block everyone coming and going. It was the last space. If you cycled there you would need to have hung your bike from a tree.

The coffee shop is tucked away down a short path from the car park. A quaint, stone built cottage with white multi-paned windows frames and a courtyard of wooden tables and benches. They use part of the building as an art gallery. Parasols were up on some tables giving a flash of red. We went inside to order coffee and cake and were pleasantly surprised by the delicious looking choices. Despite being remote the pantry and coolers were stuffed with good food. I needn't have worrried if the road back to Tobermory collapsed and we ended up stuck there for a month.

We sat outside in the sun to sip our coffee and demolish our cake. Both were worth waiting for. My only reservation in telling you this is the next time I go there will be nowhere to park and I will have to turn around and go back to Tobermory.

The friendly service and delicious offerings were delightful, but it got even better. Blue Tits darted around the tables looking for a crumb. I obliged with a piece of carrot cake and several of them descended on it in a flurry. Before long, our new-found friends put their skittishness to the side and perched on my boot to peck at the tidbits. One of them got gallus enough to land on our table where it nibbled on a thumb sized piece of cake. It was such an agreeable experience.

Smiling, we returned to the car and drove up to have a look at Glengorm Castle. Glengorm Castle is a 19th-century country house. A castellated Scottish baronial style mansion with a flourish of towers and turrets. The castle was the idea of John Forsyth of Quinnish (sounds like some drunk Scot came up with that name). The story goes that Forsyth cleared the crofters from the area by bullying them and burning their houses to make way for him to build Glengorm Castle. One old crofter woman produced deeds that entitled her to the land but Forsyth threw the titles into the fire and gave her seven days to get off her own land.

Forsyth returned seven days later and found the woman had enlisted the help of the local minister. Together they produced the original title deeds to her small property. Forsyth was fuming mad. So he built a fence around her cottage to prevent her and anyone else from coming or going. The siege was on, he intended to starve her out. Only that didn't work. The old woman had many friends and at night men would climb the cliffs at the back of Mishnish Estate and sneak provisions to her. She got her revenge too. The old woman cursed Forysth and made it known to him that he would never live in the place. It was eerily prophetic as John Forsyth of Quinnish died just days before Glengorm Castle was completed.

A sign just outside the front lawn of Glengorm Castle informed us we were on private land. The castle is now split into apartments and used as self catering holiday lets or as a wedding venue. I detoured to the left and parked outside the large vegetable garden. We went back up to the castle to a get a picture then Mrs McEwan went for a wander around the grounds.

"I think they like their privacy, going by the signs."

"Och, if someone comes out we will just tell them we are interested in hiring the whole place for our 25th wedding anniversary."

A cunning plan.

We sauntered up the side of the mansion and out to the back. It was beautiful. The views from the back were truly impressive. Green fields rolled down to the cliffs and walking paths were just visible, identifiable by the darker shade of grass. I hoped someone would come out and question us, in the off chance we might get a peek inside. Nobody came to chase us away, so we didn't get to execute our plan.

We headed back to our hotel. Content that we had had an excellent day out and wishing we could have stayed another day to explore the rest of the island. When I go back to Mull I want to walk on the white sands of Calgary Beach, see the view from the top of Ben More, and stand on the Strait of Erraid as the tide comes in to separate the rocky outcrop from the rest of Mull. I might even relive my youth and visit Iona or take a boat trip to the small island of Staffa to marvel at Fingal's cave.

Back at our hotel, we had a nice dinner, a six course taster menu, and we supped wine. At the table next to us were a group of eight Frenchmen jabbering away in their native language.

I am not gifted in languages. I wonder if learning languages is like learning a musical instrument, in that you need to have an inbred ability to pick up the nuances? I sat my 'O' grade French at school. I did a crash course in it in my sixth year. My translation from English to French was utterly abysmal, however, I filled in the gaps in my knowledge translating French to English using an educated guess and thus scraped a 'C' pass. Thus I could never call myself multi-lingual.

My number one son came home from primary school with homework; a list of words that he had to find rhyming words for.

1. Yellow
2. Boat
3. Figure
4. Heard

"Dad, can you help me?" he asked.

"What have you got so far?"

"I've got 'mellow' for yellow, 'coat' for 'boat' but I can't think of anything that rhymes with 'figure' or 'heard.'"

"Yup, that's quite difficult. What about saying 'figure' rhymes with 'trigger.'"

"Thanks dad. What about 'heard?'"

"Hm, that is a hard one. Why don't you write 'heard' rhymes with the French word 'merde.'"

"Brilliant, thanks, Dad."

At the next parents evening the head mistress called me into her office and sat me down in a small chair, told me to hold my hand out and she spanked me with a ruler. It was at that point I found out my French was even worse than I thought. I genuinely thought 'merde' meant 'murder.' The head mistress informed me that wasn't the case.

NB: 'Merde' is the French swear word for 'shit.'

I blame the teachers, I mean what else rhymes with 'heard?' Nothing, not a thing. Not unless you can use a French expletive.

My embarrassment was complete, and I consigned myself to the belief that I was useless at learning languages. However, a few years ago we had a family holiday to the South of France. It turned out to be one of the best holidays we ever had. France is beautiful. If it wasn't for speaking an incomprehensible language I might want to spend more time there.

So I set myself a goal. I would teach myself to speak French. How hard can it really be if I put my mind to it?

I downloaded an App to my phone and did five minutes a day learning new words and phrases. Because it was like a game, I soon increased to ten and sometimes twenty minutes practice. When I took the dog for a walk, instead of listening to music, I listened to a French podcast lesson. I also wanted to go to Italy, so I did Italian as well. Every day I'd work my way through the App in French and then in Italian. I'd listen to French and Italian on the podcast on alternate days. I did this for a full year with the intention of going to France and Italy and being able to hold my own in any situation. Then I added Portuguese to my list. It slowed my progress, I have to admit, but I wanted to at least have the basics. It seems only polite to be able to say 'please' and 'thank you' in someone's birth language when you are in their country.

The very next year my wife suggested we go to Lanzarote.

"Lanzagrotty," I spat back at her, "I don't want to go there I want to go to France and speak French, drink their wine and eat their cheeses. I'd like to tour right through France and on into Italy and drink their wine and eat pasta. I don't want to go to Lanzagrotty."

"Well, I want to relax in an all inclusive."

So we compromised and booked an all-inclusive in Lanzagrotty.

I added Spanish to my list of languages.

Within days I had confused myself so much I gave up. All my language learning fell by the wayside. Even learning any more French seemed pointless.

But there I was, content with my six course dinner in my belly, washed down with nice wine and a group of Frenchmen at the next table. It was time I got some practice with my French. On the way out of the restaurant I stopped at their table.

"Bonjour," I said, "comment allez vous?"

There was a barrage of Francais fired at me by all eight Frenchmen and I couldn't pick out anything anyone said.

"Excuse moi. Mon Francais c'est tres mauvais. Parlez lentement s'il vous plait. Aussi un personne seulemont."

One of the Frenchies became their spokesperson and talked in English. His English was decidedly better than my French.

"Ah, good evening. Your French is not bad but you do not need to speak in French we can all speak English."

"Mais oui, j'aime apprendre Francais. Comment votre repas?"

Asking how they enjoyed their meal set them off again. All eight talked at once. Some in English, some in French. It appeared I had touched a raw nerve. For me dinner had been perfectly agreeable. I was interested in what they thought of our Scottish fare. They were not happy.

"Zut alors! C'est terrible."

"Nous avons du attendre une heure entre les cours."

"Le repas n'etait pas bon."

"Je ne servais pas cette nouriture à un chien en France."

I got the gist. They didn't enjoy their meal.

The food was not tasty enough for them and the service was deplorable, having waited a half hour between courses. They had a cheek, have you ever eaten in a restaurant in France and not missed the last bus home? Their onslaught of complaints continued as if I were to blame. Faced with overwhelming odds I pulled out my white flag, which was ironic considering who I was speaking to.

"I better leave you in peace," I said, then in an inspired piece of retribution I shook each of the French guests by hand and said, "Cheerio, ya dunderheid."

Halfway through one of them asked, "What is this you say?"

"Cheerio, ya dunderheid. It is a Scottish term of endearment. We say it all the time to people we like."

And with that ticking time bomb, I left them. As soon as I was out of sight I had a little giggle to myself and imagined the confusion when they checked out in the morning.

I was sad to leave Mull. It is a wonderful island a little gem of a place. Not only did I want to go back sometime, but I also had a hankering to visit more islands on the west coast of Scotland.

I drove off the ferry at Oban in third place. Most of the hundreds of vehicles behind me would end up on the same road I was going, so I decided not to stop and buy more salmon and prawn sandwiches at the shack on the pier. I could get a clear run from third place. Any further back on the ferry and my advice would be to get off the ferry, park up and go to the shack. Let all the caravans and camper vans go. Have a leisurely sandwich for they are just the best.

Chapter fifteen

WHAT'S IT CALLED?

"Scotland has been voted the most beautiful country in the world," I told Mike as we sipped our beers, keen to extol the virtues of exploring Scotland.

"Well, whoever voted in that poll has never been to Rumford."

I laughed. Mike was probably right, Rumford sounds awful.

We were on a night out, and our conversation had turned towards our travels, Mike regaled me with all the wonderful places he had been. Exotic places like Majorca, Malaga, and Marbella. So I accepted his word on that.

A few days later I got to wondering if what he said was fair. Was Rumford so bad?

I consulted with the font of all knowledge; *'Rumford is a small village in Falkirk Area Council with a population of around 421.'* Google informed me.

I found *Rumford Cottages - holidaycottages.co.uk,* but this site advertised holiday cottages in Devon. The tiny village of Rumford, Devon looked quaint. There was nothing like that for Rumford, Scotland.

I discovered there is such a thing as a *Rumford fireplace*, nothing to do with Rumford the town but named after Count Rumford, a physicist who investigated the best way to heat a room and streamline the smoke away.

Rumford has a public library, I discovered, only to have my delight dashed as I realised there are at least three Rumfords' in the world and the one with the public library is in Maine, United States. *Rumford, Maine* is a run-down industrial town, and on *Google Earth,* it look rather tawdry.

So is there anything nice I can say about Rumford, Scotland? I took a trip to the other side of Falkirk to see for myself.

Rumford, I found, is tiny. It has the population of a small hotel. If I blinked, I might have missed it. However, it has nice houses and it doesn't look like a bad place to stay. At one end is *'Scottish Touch'* a kilt hire and gift shop. They even have a website (which promises to be back online very soon).

Rumford might not have very much in the way of shops or play parks or viewpoints, but it is perfectly pleasant. Now Cumbernauld... is a different matter.

Cumbernauld might have two twinned towns, but it also has a suicide pact with Beirut. Scientists suggested an experiment, instead of putting lifetime sentence offenders in prison, they should open Scotland's Secret Bunker, shove them in and lock the door. They already tried that - that's how we ended up with Cumbernauld.

Just kidding.

What really happened was a committee got together and designed a car park in Glasgow. However, forty lorries carrying the concrete had a pile-up on the East side of Glasgow and the result was Cumbernauld.

Cumbernauld is like Marmite; you either like it or you don't. (I once won a lifetime supply of Marmite - one jar). You often meet people who have come from Cumbernauld but never meet anyone who is going. Cumbernauld, they say, has nothing to look at but the traffic on the M80. Spare a thought for those travelling on the M80, who have nothing to look at but Cumbernauld.

What about the people of Cumbernauld?

My Uncle Will is from Cumbernauld; he joined *Facebook* just so he could post the words, 'Leave me alone!'

My disdain for Cumbernauld started when I saw their TV advertising campaign in the 1980s. Their tagline became, *'What's it called - Cumbernauld.'* The campaign tried to entice people to live in the area. This highlights my point, anyone who has to advertise their town is on a losing end of smack in the face, aren't they?

Despite only being designated as a site for a new town in 1955, Cumbernauld is now the ninth most populous town in Scotland, so they must have done something right - right?

I wasn't sure.

To dispel any myths about the place and to rein in any further jokes that might offend a 'Cumbernauldian,' (Is that what we call you if you come from Cumbernauld?) I thought I had better go there.

Before going, I did my research.

I found articles such as, *'Cumbernauld isn't crap, and here's a list of reasons why...'* The author, Scott Campbell, explained himself with a list of twenty-six reasons.

No.1 reason: It is home to the first indoor shopping mall.

Yeah, but that indoor shopping mall is a train-wreck, Scott. It might have free parking, but it looks like the same guy who invented shipping containers designed it. It might be okay once you are inside but from the outside, it is a lifeless, dreary eyesore.

No. 2 reason: Bill Forsyth used Cumbernauld as the backdrop to his cult Scottish film *'Gregory's Girl.'*

Yeah, Scott, Bill's decision to use Cumbernauld was deliberate, he wanted as drab, dull, and dowdy a backdrop as he could find.

Gregory's Girl is a film about a boy who tries to date Dorothy, a good looking lass and the schools best footballer. He arranges to meet her, but she doesn't show. Instead, Gregory ends up going on a series of dates with other girls from his school. Gregory doesn't end up with Dorothy, but he finds happiness. Thanks to the advice of his younger sister Madeline he ends up with Susan, who has had a thing for Gregory from the outset. The film was a box office smash, and it catapulted images of Cumbernauld around the world to an eager audience. The film even broke records at the Dominion Cinema in Edinburgh where it played continually for three years. Did it make the world want to go there? Well, no! It just made people want to watch the film. Fans want to go to the restaurant in *'When Harry Met Sally'* or the bookshop in *'Notting Hill.'* They don't want to visit an underpass in Cumbernauld. The film featured the real Abronhill High School and used many of its pupils as extras. You can't even visit that school anymore; North Lanarkshire Council demolished it in 2014 as part of a cost-cutting exercise.

No. 7 reason: In 2012 Cumbernauld was named the 'Best Town' at the Scottish Design Awards.

Okay, fair enough. In an online survey, Cumbernauld came top in a public poll for civic pride. It narrowly beat Peebles, a town with a population of just over 8,000 and I suspect just under 8,000 of them were unaware they could vote on such a thing.

I also note, Cumbernauld has the distinction of winning the 'Plook on the Plinth' titles in 2001 and 2005, in the Carbuncle awards, for having the most dismal town centre in Scotland. Judges described its shopping centre as a rabbit warren on stilts and compared the town to Kabul.

The question is, why would I include Cumbernauld here? This book is very much about the best that Scotland offers, my number one places to go, so why even mention it?

It crossed my mind that for any nation to earn the title of 'most beautiful country in the world' it has to do so by dragging up the worst places. There has to be an average. You can only be as good as the worst man in your team. I bet there are green pastured valleys and picturesque mountain lakes in Afghanistan that are not representative of our images of the place as a whole. That doesn't mean you would want to go there. Conversely, there will be idyllic islands in the Caribbean that have festering spots of detritus I might not want to see, but that wouldn't put me off enjoying a two-week break in Jamaica, drinking rum and swimming in the sea.

So I visited Cumbernauld to see for myself, I got in the car and took, what I imagined to be, the road to hell.

The good thing about Cumbernauld is that it has lots of car parks surrounding its town centre. The bad thing about Cumbernauld is that it has lots of car parks surrounding its town centre. As an outsider, I had no idea where was the best place to park. I took the road through the middle, which splits the shopping centre in two. There was nothing imagined about its unpleasantness. I felt more welcome the time I trailed dog turd through my Dentist's surgery - not the first time he turned his nose up at me.

At the far end, I took a right and ended up turning back on myself, heading in the same direction I had just come, but skirting the rear of the buildings. There is even less there to greet the eye. I passed a windowless discount store and a building that looked like a single massive freight container with a glass door. The sign said 'freedom city church centre' I prayed I would never have to cross its doorstep.

The next windowless monstrosity advertised itself as a 'roller disco' - what fun. Seconds later I was under the town centre, a ghastly building on stilts that reminded me of some suburb of Moscow I'd seen in a black and white film set in the 1950s. And I still didn't know where to park.

I ended up back where I started and had to double back around a small roundabout and follow signpost that took me up a steep ramp to the roof car park. I parked and alighted. Large corrugated boxes that looked like they covered the gubbins behind the heating systems were spaced out in front of a row of shops. The building seemed to have been built inside out. It is distinctly uninviting. I looked for the way into the main shopping mall and headed towards the only doors I could see. Instead of leading me into the building it took me out to a walkway bridge that crossed the main road. Since there was nothing to entice me to stay on the side I was on, I crossed it. I went down a spiral staircase and found myself in another car park. Not sure of which way to go I plodded toward a small sign attached to a wall above a dark alleyway. It said;

'Welcome to Cumbernauld Town Centre'

It would have felt more welcoming if they poured hot tar on me from the roof. It was like walking into a street tunnel from *'The Warriors.'* If it had been raining I would have said *'Blade Runner.'* If dark woods surrounded this place, then I'm sure I would have heard a banjo dual playing in the background. I was torn between going in and getting my head kicked in or running back to my car in the hope it was still there and would start first time.

I plucked up the courage and entered. The lack of any signage indicating I was on the right path was disconcerting. Then I saw a lift. I was in the right place after all. The sign on the lift said I was on the ground floor (Parking Red 2), I could use the lift to go to floor *'1 - no access'*, floor *'2 - shopping level,'* floor *'3 - Avon House, Library, Nursery'* or floor *'4 - no access'*. So I got in the lift. I wanted to go to floor *'2 - shopping level.'*

I looked for a push button for level 2. There wasn't any. Every other floor had a button I could press. There was no button for floor two. I couldn't press one or four because there was no access and I didn't want to go to level 3. I had no choice but to get out again and march all the way to the other end of the building and go up via a walkway that doubled back on itself. It brought me out into the 'Town Centre.'

I wish I hadn't bothered.

Cumbernauld Town Centre sits inside an elongated shipping container on stilts. From the outside it is bleak and uninviting, on the inside it is just as depressing. I had a quick scan and concluded that the best shops had 'To Let' signs. A charity project occupied two sides of the mall, and it looked like people had emptied a skip through their front doors. One member of staff stood in the middle of some junk wondering what to do with it all, another fat bloke sat at a computer, ignoring all the mess around him, playing solitaire.

I looked for the way out.

A sign directed me towards the 'Antonine Shopping Centre'. An escalator took me down one level. The mid-level had a large alcove on the right, nothing else. The alcove was filled with fruit machines, a couple of pool tables, one 'throw the ball into the basket' game - but mainly it was filled with fruit machines. The multi-coloured lights flashed and bells sounded in the mistaken belief they might attract some of my hard earned money. The place looked empty; I wondered if people now realised these places only amused the persons who emptied the machines of their coins.

Then something moved.

The arcade wasn't empty. A man sidled zombielike from one bandit to another, his hand went to his pocket and dug around until he retrieved the last of his loose change. I heard the clatter of silver cascading into a metal tray, and I spotted another addict, a haggard-faced woman, she had hit the jackpot. Even this didn't seem to entertain her. Unsmiling, her hand dipped into the tray, and as fast as she could, she removed her winnings and inserted them back into the slot at the top. I moved on before the desperation crept up on me and dragged me into the same self-destructive mood.

I descended the last set of stairs and came out into the middle of the mall. The Antonine Shopping Centre is moderately better than Cumbernauld Town Centre. It was busier, had a better variety of shops and didn't have any empty units. Still, it was as unappealing as a four-day-old ham sandwich. I marched up to one end and back down to the other until I found what I was looking for - an exit. To get there, I had to walk through *'Dunnes Store,'* (Fashion, Homewares, Gifts & More). Kevin Bridges once described *Dunnes* as the midway point between *Primark* and shoplifting; it was hard to disagree.

I didn't dawdle.

Outside I found my bearings and headed back towards the spiral staircase that would take me up to the walkway back to my car. I thought I was doing well until some Heras fencing scuppered my intent. I had to backtrack fifty yards to get around. That niggled me when I realised the fencing served no purpose. I cursed under my breath. Why would they put fencing up for no reason? There wasn't any work going on. It just prevented people from taking the most direct route out of the place. Just one more exasperating thing about Cumbernauld that would put off from ever coming back. My frustration didn't end there.

I started up my car and couldn't wait to get out of the place, only to find the car park is the single worst sign-posted car park I have ever had the misfortune to enter. When I eventually found the exit, I discovered that anything less than a 4X4 jeep struggles to negotiate the speed bumps. These were more like playthings for mountain goats. Anyone with a low slung sports car would have to abandon it or risk ripping their sump to shreds.

When I did eventually escape, I parked up at the side of the road and did some mindfulness breathing. I closed my eyes and imagined myself in some far-flung Caribbean island, Guantanamo Bay came to mind, and it was still miles better than Cumbernauld Town Centre.

There must be more to Cumbernauld than its Town Centre, I thought.

Cumbernauld's history extends all the way back to Roman times. To the north-east is an area called Westerwood. Westerwood was the site of a Roman Fort. The fort sat on the Antonine Wall, the northernmost frontier of the Roman Empire. The Antonine wall stretches forty miles from the Firth of Clyde to the Firth of Forth. It took twelve years for the Romans to build. Eight years after they had completed it the Romans couldn't be bothered with the hassle and fell back to Hadrian's Wall. I drove a mile and a half up the dual carriageway, under the M80 and arrived at Westerwood.

Westerwood Hotel and Golf Course opened in 1989. In contrast to the lacklustre town centre of Cumbernauld, the Hotel is modern and chic. It has an award-winning spa that cost over half a million pounds to build. Seve Ballesteros designed the course which undulates over moorland greens with beautiful views of the Campsie Hills. It has one of the most tricky par three holes in Scotland. The 'Waterfall Hole,' has an elevated tee and green surrounded by a 20-metre high rock face and a risky little burn that sweeps across the front bunker. I'm not sure it is all that fair on Westerwood to say it is part of Cumbernauld.

I got out and wandered up to the first tee. The lay of the land is such that the course dips away out of sight. Eighteen testing holes of golf with Cumbernauld nowhere to be seen. What's not to like? Unfortunately, it was February when I visited, the only thing that put me off going for a daunder was the cold wind blowing up the valley. It made me shudder, so I returned to the relative warmth of my car.

On route to Westerwood, I had seen a tourist information sign giving directions to *'Cumbernauld Theatre'* so I backtracked down the dual carriageway and went to investigate. The road to *Cumbernauld Theatre* is a single track road made of pot-holes and weeds. It brought me out into an empty car park, and I took a second to realise that Cumbernauld Theatre is just a row of converted cottages with emulsioned white walls and black shutters over the windows and doors. I'm sure it is a perfectly suitable venue for tribute bands or any interactive arty farty stuff. Since getting there requires a car and I would need to be drunk to make it through any performance, I don't see myself ever making it over the doorstep.

It was time to head home.

The one-way system made me drive up the dual carriageway again back to the Town Centre and circumnavigate a roundabout before I could turn back south. I was thoroughly fed up with Cumbernauld. There isn't even an efficient way to escape it.

As I made my way towards the M80, I saw a signpost for Cumbernauld Village. On a whim, I switched on my indicator and turned off to have a look. More by chance than intention I ended up in a car park at the back of the Main Street. The Cumbernauld Village Main Street looks more like a traditional town centre. It has a pub, a Chinese takeaway, a flower shop, and a bakery. All the shops and stores you might expect in a small village. It even has an independent coffee shop; *Ruffles Coffee House* is no Starbucks, Costa Coffee or Café Nero, and thank goodness. I was hungry and thirsty, so I popped in. I found a comfortable seat in the corner and examined the menu. Sandwiches and soup or toasted sandwiches and soup, nothing pretentious here. It was a basic menu at reasonable prices.

I ordered a coffee and a toastie, before taking in my surroundings.

The cafe looked worn but homely. Small circular tables seated four, except at one side where a padded window seat catered for more. A group of twenty-somethings had taken up residence. Their resemblance to the cast of *Friends* was uncanny. Chandler Bing was the geeky guy with glasses. He made quick-witted comments that made the group burst into fits of giggles. Ross sat awkwardly in the window seat and occasionally his eyes would glaze over as if his mind had taken him someplace else. Joey sprawled in his seat, legs akimbo, he took a second or two longer to get Chandler's jokes but when he did he let out a bellowing guffaw.

Phoebe sat, mobile phone in hand looking goofy. Monica smiled while she wiped the table with a napkin. Their conversation turned to Rachael, the sixth member of their group was missing. Monica leaned in to impart gossip, and the rest of the group followed suit. I leaned closer too.

"You won't believe it," whispered Monica.

"What?"

"Rachael has gone and done it."

"What, what has she done?" Ross blurted all too eagerly.

"You have to keep this to yourselves."

"Okay, okay, what is it?" Joey pushed.

"Guys, this is huge. I don't know if I should tell you this. I should let her tell you herself."

"You need to tell us now!" Ross berated.

"Phoebe agreed, "You can't keep it a secret now you have said something."

"All right, I'll tell you, but none of you better spill the beans - I never told you."

"Promise, cross my heart hope to die," Ross was still too eager.

"Rachael..."

"C'mon, Rachael what?"

"Rachael is pregnant."

"You're kidding!"

"Wow, seriously?"

"Who too?"

"No way!"

Phoebe put her phone up to her ear. She had been dialling Rachael's number.

"Rachael, we just heard, congratulations," there was a slight pause, "no Monica just told us."

Monica looked shocked, and the rest of them burst out laughing.

I smiled to myself and had a look around at the other punters.

Diagonally opposite were two old ladies eating their soup. They chatted so enthusiastically and loud that every single word could be heard clearly by the lady under the hairdryer in the hairdressers across the road. One, in particular, could have been gainfully employed as a foghorn. They took a sup of their soup and then gossiped for two or three minutes before taking another sip. Their bowls lasted the whole time I took to sit down, order, get served, eat, drink, read a chapter of my book, pay and leave. They might have been better ordering the gazpacho than the lentil.

A couple in their mid-fifties sat at another table. Unlike most couples of that age, they weren't looking at each other like they were to blame for all their life's ills. They were enjoying each other's company. She seductively sipped her coffee, and his eyes stayed on hers. They were clearly in love. It was nice to see a happy couple comfortable in growing old together.

I enjoyed my cappuccino, and my toastie was satisfying. It wasn't *Central Perk,* but it had a nice feel to it. My server, a cheery middle-aged blonde lady, couldn't have been nicer. It wasn't just the hot coffee that warmed my belly, it was the convivial atmosphere.

It was at that moment I realised what I had missed about Cumbernauld.

Yes, the Town Centre is utterly characterless, and the road network is a pain in the backside. Of that, there is no doubt. What I hadn't done was engage with the people. The nice thing about Cumbernauld, I discovered, are its inhabitants. Cumbernauld's real success story is that it has prospered despite the horrible design. Do not judge it on that alone.

Cumbernauld is all about the vibrant community and their spirit. It is a friendly, decent place to bring up a family. It doesn't matter that the buildings are the stuff of post-apocalyptic nightmares. The townsfolk make the most of it, they are happy and sociable. Listening to them in the cafe made me want to be a part of their conversations. I imagine it is their spirit as a community that the people of Cumbernauld voted for in the online poll. They are full of civic pride and they deserve their award. If they can put up with their town centre and still come out smiling then they have earned it.

So don't visit Cumbernauld - go live there. Or get a copy of *Gregory's Girl* and watch that. It is a feel good movie about a feel good place.

Chapter sixteen

DON'T GO NEAR THE WATER

"Strewth Bruce, will ya look at the size of those Kelpies."

Bruce spread apart the corks dangling from his hat as if opening a curtain.

"Kelpies? Sheila, they look just like horses."

"Well I'll be a waltzing Matilda in a goolagong if you ain't got that right Bruce."

Their voices grated. Not because of the thick Australian accents but because of their volume. I was having a quiet walk along the canal bank, Monkeydog at my side heading towards the Kelpies and had been halted in my tracks by the couple taking up the width of the towpath in front. Shiela's ears were plugged and wired to a Sony Walkman secured to the belt on her hip - the volume just loud enough to pick out Kylie Minogue's sweet-sounding voice. She obviously couldn't hear me coming up behind her and neither could Bruce who, I presumed from his foghorn tone, was a little deaf.

The Kelpies are one hundred feet high horse-head sculptures at the north end of Falkirk. They stand next to the Forth and Clyde Canal near the River Carron. Made from steel they are the largest equine structures in the world and each weigh in at over 300 tonnes. Completed in November 2013 they took over five months to construct on site. Falkirk Council reclaimed marshland next to the Kelpies and built a recreational space called 'The Helix.' They did it well. It is a pleasant place to while away an afternoon. There are several places to stop for a coffee and a bite to eat, a visitor centre, a lagoon, a play area, paths, and wetlands.

My only complaint: Falkirk Council did not believe in themselves.

They didn't appreciate how popular it would be. Car parking is therefore limited. Credit where credit is due, they put in a zebra crossing at the main road and visitors can now cross safely to use the additional parking facilities at Falkirk Football Stadium.

The Australian couple holding me up realised I was behind and stepped to the side. I took the opportunity to have a chat, my first mistake.

"Did you not know the Kelpies were horses?"

"We thought they were dogs."

"Dogs?" I queried.

"A Kelpie is a working dog."

"A working dog, like a Border Collie?"

"Not like your black and tans, we have Red Cloud Dogs. A Border Collie has too much coat. The outback is a harsh environment so we bred them to be tough. Rock hard little dogs that work all day long. Loyal too."

"Goid tempra too," chipped in Shiela.

I tried to compute what she was saying and then got the gist. They were surprised to see that the Kelpies were horses and not sheepdogs. I thought I'd better explain.

"Our Kelpies are actually mythical horses who inhabited our lochs and waterways. The Loch Ness Monster is thought to have originated as a Kelpie and shape-shifted through folklore into what people imagine him to be now. Our Falkirk Kelpies are powerful beasts with the strength of a hundred men. They are said to appear in the dusk and drag

221

lone travellers from the water's edge and devour them, tossing away their entrails. The only sign they leave are hoof prints which are back to front."

I wasn't sure if all I said was accurate but I had read something like that. A myth our ancestors made to tell their kids to prevent them going near dangerous waters on their own. That's how superstition enters our psyche.

"Strewth Bruce, that's really bad."

"Roight, Sheila. We've gotta real live one here. Mate, it's goid to meetcha."

"Yes, G'day."

"Sure that's interesting. Why don't you come on down to the caff and we'll get you a coffee and a choccy biccy."

"Good idea Bruce, we ain't had our brekky yet," Sheila smiled at me.

"Yes, why not." I agreed.

"Fair dinkum."

And off we toddled to the café.

That was my second mistake.

When I was a police sergeant a lot of my job was to do with listening. Listening to instructions, listening to the public, listening to crooks and listening to cops and all their problems. All part of the job. There I was in the café with Bruce and Sheila, sipping my coffee, listening to their inane twittering. Monkeydog stared in from outside wishing he was inside. I stared out wishing it was the other way about.

"...and you don't get anything better than Sidney Opera House anywhere in the world. Did you know Arnold Schwarzenegger won his final body building title there in, when was it Sheila?"

"Bruce, I think that was the year Kylie joined Neighbours."

"It must have been before that Sheila, when Jason was first in it."

As a sergeant there were obstacles put in my way to prevent me from doing my job. No matter how busy I was, no matter what was going on, there was always someone, a boss or an officer from another department, looking to waste my time. Someone who couldn't care less that I was run off my feet. The object of his exercise was for him to get to the end of his day doing as little work as possible. Come five o'clock, 'whoosh' he was out the door faster than the *Road Runner* on speed. It wasn't long before I developed a strategy for dealing with such time wasters.

It took a little while to perfect, but I came up with an amazing ploy. It offended no one; it cost nothing, it just made the time waster get up and go away.

If I wanted, I could use this strategy as soon as he walked in the door. Alternatively, I could just decide mid-conversation he was wasting my time. I would use the technique on him; he would stop talking and walk away. It let me get back to my work, and it would work on anyone. On a cleaner who wanted to complain about another cleaner, a boss who wanted to dump his work on me or a colleague who just wanted to chew the fat. It was the most effective tool I had.

I no longer put up with time wasting. It was a simple way of maximising my valuable time, without causing offence or creating friction. Every time I used it people simply got up and left, like magic. I think most people thought better of me

223

after I had used it too. I know you will be wondering what this powerful technique is. How does it work?

I am reluctant to tell anyone after I walked into my inspector's office one day and got chatting with him. We discussed the demands of the job, and he identified that there were several 'time wasters' in our building who were worth avoiding. He had wasted hours that morning with a certain chief inspector who was 'working' on a project.

"God knows how long the project will take him because all he seems to do is saunter around the building seeing who he can cadge a coffee from and then talk gibberish."

My inspector looked frustrated. That is when I told him I had a solution. I told him I had a technique and that my strategy worked every time. Simple and effective.

"What is it?" he asked.

So I told him.

"What I do, mid-conversation is glance at my watch or look at the clock on the wall and say, 'Oh my! Is that the time?' That get's their attention. Then I follow up with, 'Listen, you will have to excuse me, I need to phone my Mum.' It is as simple as that."

My Inspector looked at me with what could only be admiration bordering on adulation. I had given him the full unadulterated manipulation technique. He sat back and nodded, pleased with himself. He now had a beautiful and elegant solution to this problem.

"Of course, I don't leave it at that. I then pick up my phone and look at whoever is wasting my time anticipating they will leave. And they do. They get up and go. So I am not telling a lie I then phone my Mum and say, 'Mum, I am just phoning to tell you I love you.' And you know every Mum appreciates being told that."

I sat back pleased with myself for having come up with such an ingenious solution.

My inspector nodded and smiled.

He looked at me again, looked at his watch then looked back at me. Then he said, "Oh my! Is that the time?"

He went straight in and used my technique on me.

"You will have to excuse me," he said, "I need to phone my Mum."

I had no choice but to get up and walk out.

When I retired I thought I might have no further use for my technique. But here in the coffee shop with Bruce and Sheila, I decided it was time to employ it again. I drained my coffee, glanced at my watch and looked surprised.

"Oh dear. Is that the time. You will need to excuse me, I need to phone my Mum."

"No worries mate," Bruce assured me.

I got up and made a hasty exit.

The Kelpies are a marvellous design. I enjoyed walking around them again, as I chatted on the phone with my Mum. They are complex constructions and I imagine the tour that takes you inside will be interesting but I also think they are much better to view from the outside. The Kelpies are fabulous.

As is the world's first rotation boat lift.

The Falkirk Wheel, on the other side of Falkirk, is an ingenious engineering solution to the problem of transferring barges from the Forth & Clyde to the Union Canal situated more than 100 feet above. It was designed to replace a series of lock gates built in the 19th century, long since demolished in preference for housing. The Falkirk Wheel is the showpiece of the Millennium Link project where coast-to-coast navigation of the canals has been re-established for the first time in over forty years. The gondolas transferring the boats and barges carry a combined weight of 500 tonnes. That's about 100 elephants or two Ryanair jumbo jets (with their minimum baggage allowance).*

Unlike Ryanair, the Falkirk Wheel allows you extra luggage for free and you can sit where you like.

It is so finely balanced that each transfer uses the same energy it takes to boil eight kettles. Which means that when my number two son is home for the day he could shift about 1000 tonnes (he drinks a lot of tea).

It is hard to believe the Falkirk Wheel is now old enough to get married. It opened in 2002 to much fanfare and wonder. When I first took my kids they guddled about in the water play area, turned the Archimedes' screw and soaked each other, much to the wrath of their mother. When they got bored with that they bent down behind their grandmother in her wheelchair so they couldn't be seen and zoomed her about on the pavement outside the visitor centre. I still smile at the video footage; wide-eyed in fear as her mode of transport buzzed here and there, apparently with a mind of its own.

I visited recently with Mrs McEwan and Monkeydog. We were even more impressed. There is a greater variety of things to do. The basin of the Falkirk Wheel is now a hub of activities: Water Walkers (those big clear balls you climb in and bounce across the water), Electric Boats, Bike Hire, Canoe Hire, Segways and Lazer Quest. All brilliant diversions for children (including the grown up variety). We recalled the nonsense our kids got up to as we sat at a table with coffee, hotdogs and a shared portion of chips. Monkeydog's eyes fixed on the hotdog in the hope of getting a bite.

The Falkirk Wheel is connected to the Kelpies by four miles of canal. The towpath is flat and weed free, solar lights are imbedded in the tarmac to give walkers a clear view of the path at night. There are sculptures and information boards along the way.

I have barely scratched the surface. However, I have just checked my watch and it is time to phone my Mum.

You will have to excuse me.

Chapter seventeen

WHAT A LOT OF BALLACHULISH

Of all the glens in Scotland, Glencoe is the grandest and most awe-inspiring. Macauley's *History* details it in all its glory:

"In the Gaelic tongue Glencoe signifies the Glen of Weeping; and in truth, that pass is the most dreary and melancholy of all the Scottish passes - the very Valley of the Shadow of Death. Mists and storms brood over it through the greater part of the finest summer; and even on those rare days when the sun is bright, and when there is no cloud in the sky, the impression made by the landscape is sad and awful. The path lies along a stream which issues from the most sullen and gloomy of mountain pools. Huge precipices of naked stone frown on both sides. Even in July the streaks of snow may often be discerned in the rifts near the summits. All down the sides of the crags heaps of ruin mark the headlong paths of the torrents."

Global warming made an appearance in Scotland during the summer and bequeathed a run of clear skies. We had twelve uninterrupted weeks of glorious sunshine. This was unheard of in Scotland. *'If you don't like the weather in Scotland - wait twenty minutes'* was a phrase I hadn't heard in weeks.

I mean this was seriously warm. People were forgetting where they left their brollies. We actually left the house without an anorak; even when we didn't know if we would be back before dark. Don't get me wrong, women still went to communion in a big woolly coat - it wasn't so hot that it warmed up the inside of a church.

I took Mrs McEwan and Monkeydog away for a few days on a leisurely trip to the west coast. Following a route through the Trossachs, we had fish and chips for lunch at the dog friendly *Real Food Café*, Tyndrum, which was delicious. Before carrying on we crossed the road to *The Green Welly Stop* and purchased the obligatory anti-midge spray (my goodness that place is busy).

At the viewpoint overlooking Loch Tulla I pulled into the layby and parked facing the black waters, Mrs McEwan and I sat spellbound and enchanted. A solitary cloud cast a shadow on the loch taking the shine off the surface where it fell, making it opaque and ominous. It slithered across the water like a malevolent presence, a shape-changing spirit. It drew us into our own thoughts. We sat in silence for many minutes.

To the east is Glen Lyon, steeped in folklore it is described as the most beautiful Scottish glen. It runs for thirty-four miles, making it the longest enclosed valley in Scotland. Deep in the glen, there is a small hut where several stones rest. Roughly shaped into human forms, then battered by the elements, the stones are water-worn and eroded. The stones symbolise the family of Cailleach, the divine hag, a goddess of our ancestors and creator of the weather. The Queen of Winter. Traditionally, the local people walked up the glen to take the Cailleach and her stone family out of their shelter at the start of the Celtic festival marking summer. Then at the end of summer (Halloween) they returned the stones back to their modest home.

In legend, Cailleach could harness the wild powers of nature, move mountains, send boulders tumbling, and raise fearsome windstorms. In fury, Cailleach could use her great powers to destroy all that lay in her path. It wasn't hard to imagine that little shadow bubbling across the water as Cailleach smouldering underneath, lying in wait for the time she could unleash her destructive power.

My mind snapped back to attention when we were disturbed by a horde of leather-clad devils. A group of loud German tourists marched past either side of our car and then stood in front of us blocking our view. Oblivious to their rudeness they barked at each other in their guttural language, an assault on our eyes and ears. It felt like they'd dropped a vial of Novichok in the car - certainly they got on my nerves. I started up my car and put it in reverse, only to find seven open topped BMW Z4s blocking my exit. Abandoned in a format not unlike like the starting grid of a Formula 1 race. I'd been so absorbed in the view I hadn't realised these were the cars the Germans had come from. The convoy had rolled to a stop without regard for anyone else.

I can be as patient as the next man, I was in no hurry but the Fritzes got my back up. I inched the Jag back until I was close enough to a Z4 for the owner to look around with some concern. Then I put it in neutral and pummeled the accelerator so that my big cat growled in anger. They soon moved.

Perhaps torrential rain and anoraks are a small price to pay for travelling undisturbed through this beautiful landscape.

My little rebuke for the German tourists was tame compared to what went on in olden times. This wild and barren part of the country once belonged to a branch of the clan Macdonald. When William III became sovereign, his ascension didn't please everyone and among the discontented were the Highlanders. William III insisted all his British subjects demonstrate their loyalty to him and the Highlanders screwed up their faces.

A demand for allegiance is a weak basis for loyalty. A tool of the Mafia, dictators, Donald Trump, and Jose Mourinho. Such loyalty is born of fear and has fragile roots. In 1691 the government required the clans to take an oath of allegiance to their new king. All submitted except the clansmen of Glencoe. Their chief, Maclan, an old man, held out to the last day. Then, realising the folly of resistance, he hastened to Fort William to take the oath, but there was no magistrate in the garrison to receive it. The nearest was at Inveraray, he hurried there to meet the deadline, but the mountain passes were deep with snow, and he missed the closing date. This wasn't like missing out on a Rod Stewart concert, this was serious.

Despite having missed the deadline, the magistrate took Chief Maclan to his chambers and administered the oath, and notified the fact to the authorities at Edinburgh. However, the magistrate's explanation of Maclan's delay didn't reach the King's advisers, the messengers to the King were enemies of the clan and sought vengeance for past deeds done. Those enemies sought authority to obtain a royal warrant to uproot the clan and do away with them forever.

William sent one hundred and twenty soldiers to Glencoe under the charge of Captain Robert Campbell. The

Campbells and Macdonalds weren't exactly the best of friends up until then - some still hold a grudge today. They entered the glen under a plausible pretext, and old Chief Maclan, suspecting no wicked intent, treated them with Highland hospitality. For twelve days they entertained, fed, and watered the soldiers, who smiled and played with their children.

At five o'clock on the morning of February 13, the massacre began. The old, the young, men, women, and children were indiscriminately slain. Those who escaped the sword fled to the hills where almost all froze to death among the rocks. When the slaughter was over, the troops looted the deserted huts before setting them on fire. The soldiers departed, driving before them the flocks and herds and Highland ponies that had belonged to the clan.

Today clusters of green mounds and grey stones mark the sites of the ruined huts. A gruesome reminder of the evil men can do in the name of a king.

Aye, ye didnae want tae fall oot wi anyone in those days.

Driving the road to Glencoe is the gift that keeps on giving. It traverses the Great Moor of Rannoch, a vast stretch of land composed of blanket bogs, rivulets, and rocky outcrops. For being in the Scottish Highlands, Rannoch Moor is strangely level. It sits in a soggy dish of granite and if it weren't for the smooth road it would be like crossing a vast bowl of chunky porridge oats.

The road rose out of the moor, up the lip of the bowl and at the top we arrived at Glencoe under a canopy of bright blue with a blazing sun at our backs and thought Macaulay prone to exaggeration. He may well have thought the glen most impressive when viewed amid mists and storms. On all but the gloomiest of days, it is a very fine sight. However, in sunlight reminiscent of that found in the Mediterranean I was taken by its grandeur. Matchless, in my opinion.

I took a detour to Glen Etive in a search for the iconic view from the James Bond film Skyfall where M (Dame Judi Dench) and Bond (Daniel Craig) stood with backs to the camera gazing at the glen below. Instead of an Aston Martin in the foreground and low clouds swirling in the deep glen, I snapped a picture of the Jag to the fore and a line of traffic stuttering to a halt in the distance as tourists swarmed the dusty road ahead.

I suppose we have to blame all those authors who buff the emotional longings of foreigners (and even our own country's city dwellers) to dispense with slippers, put on a sturdy pair of hiking boots and take to the hills. It is they who are causing our tranquil spots in magical glens to flood with photo-bombers.

We stopped at various spots to walk Monkeydog and take a snap of him sitting in the foreground of a majestic hill, all regal like a lion, (not a bad look for a mongrel terrier). Finding a place without a bright yellow anorak in the background or a family standing on every headland was hard. We tried walking further afield only to come across another group and then another. Or someone would pop up behind us and ask us to move out of their picture.

Sightseeing is like a nice bottle of malt whisky. You don't want to drink it all in the one go. You want to savour it. A little nip at a time, on special occasions: Christmas, birthdays, or Rangers beating Celtic. And like a nice bottle of malt, sightseeing is always better when shared. All good things in life are better when shared.

Scotland will never be so teeming with tourists you can't enjoy it in peace at some time of the year. Visiting Scotland isn't like standing in a queue at Disneyland, you don't have to wait in a line for two hours to see the attractions. The views are just there. On most occasions you are going to get a bit of rain and all those fair-weather folk will disappear, leaving you to your quiet thoughts.

On Scotland's magnificent west coast superhighway of the sea, between the Sound of Mull and Oban, Loch Linnhe cradles the Isle of Lismore and extends north where it enters a narrow inlet and turns east, passing underneath the iron bridge between North Ballachulish and South Ballachulish. There it opens out to become Loch Leven. From its mouth to its farthest extremity Loch Leven presents an unbroken succession of grand and romantic landscapes. This sea loch widens at the village of Glencoe then tapers all the way to Kinlochleven, the penultimate stop for walkers on the West Highland Way.

I booked us into the *Isles of Glencoe Hotel* built on a thumb shaped promontory that pokes out into Loch Leven. The hotel is in the village of Ballachulish and not the village of Glencoe, where I presumed it might be. Then again, the village of Ballachulish is two miles away from the bridge that connects North Ballachulish and South Ballachulish.

Confused? You will be with the next episode of 'What a lot of Ballachulish.'

The *Isles of Glencoe Hotel* is in an idyllic spot, despite being built on the workings of a giant slate mine. The old quarry supplied most of Scotland with slate for generations. Ballachulish slate is prized the world over as a roofing material, all the more since the mines closed. The slate quarry, opposite the hotel, is now a monument to the men who built the Scottish slate industry, and where you can see huge natural sculptures by the side of still ponds.

We parked up, checked in and were shown to our room overlooking the small island of Eilean Munde. Eilean Munde is the site of a chapel built by St. Fintan Mundus and also the site of a graveyard once used by the Stewarts of Ballachulish, the Macdonalds of Glencoe, and the Camerons of Callart. The clans shared the maintenance of the graveyard, even when there was a conflict between them. Which is a bit like Celtic, Rangers and Aberdeen fans getting together to cut the grass at Tynecastle because one day they might play there.

Behind Eilean Munde is the smaller island of Eilean a' Chombraidh, otherwise known as the Isle of Discussion, where members of the Macdonald Clan were sent by their Chief when they had an argument. They rowed the disagreeing parties out to the isle and left them there with no food or water. Only once they had resolved their differences were they allowed back to the mainland. I imagine all arguments were resolved by dusk, for no other reason than you don't want to be on a small island in a loch on the west coast of Scotland when the midges come out. For those of you who think that being scared of a tiny wee beastie like a midge is an irrational fear - I challenge you to sit in a boat on a loch when dusk falls and the wind drops.

I like this 'Isle of Discussion' idea. Arguments are an inevitable part of living together. When they happen, it is important to remember you will still have to live with that person afterwards. Thus is it okay to disagree, but it is not good to insult or offend. Focus on the present not the past. We should all consider ammunition from the past as spent. Avoid provocative words, like 'always' and 'never,' they serve only to inflame a dispute. Saying nothing can be just as bad, a willingness to say sorry is the salve that soothes and comforts.

If that doesn't work, wait until they are not looking and skelp them on the back of their heid.

We explored the grounds, had a beer on the lawn and watched a small yacht bob up and down in the inlet. We booked dinner for eight and headed back to our room to change. I switched the TV channel to the football, Brazil were playing Belgium in the World Cup and promised to be one of the better games of the tournament. Mrs McEwan isn't too keen on the football and at one point if a rowing boat had been handy, a Macdonald might have ferried us across to the Isle of Discussion and left us there.

We had reservations about dinner. When we bought drinks earlier, I asked if they had nuts or crisps and was told they hadn't had a delivery and had none left. This didn't bode well for our evening meal. If they can't get crisps or nuts, what are the chances of them having all the ingredients required for a good dinner?

Our fears weren't justified. The meal could not have been better. We sat by the big window and were served superbly presented food, which almost surpassed the spectacular views of the loch. I couldn't fault any of our three courses. It is rare for something to leave me smacking my lips - but this food did, it was so tasty.

Afterwards, to allow our dinner to digest, we took Monkeydog for a wander around the promontory again. A trail from a jet split the full length of the sky and disappeared behind the hills. As the light dimmed the jet stream changed to orange then fiery red. Monkeydog sat concentrating on a swan, like he was threading a needle. The swan swayed in the water as the tide rippled underneath it. The swell gently headed on and tickled the stony shore. Honestly, it was stunning. I defy any Scot to look at that panorama and not feel your heart thump with pride.

In the morning, we woke to calm. Our view revealed a mirror still loch. It perfectly reflected the cotton wool cirrocumulus, the green hills and the blue and white yacht standing to attention in the middle of the inlet. It was hard to pull myself away from this oasis of peace. The view was even more beautiful than the night before. It is easy to see why people fall in love with this part of Scotland.

I've said it before and I will say it again, if it wasn't for the midges...

OH GOOD YOU MADE IT TO THE END

So nice of you to read my tales. I hope you enjoyed them.

If you smiled at one or two bits, or maybe laughed out loud - great. Perhaps you learned something you didn't know about Scotland or are now tempted to visit one of the places mentioned, if that is the case then my job here is done.

CLUNK (sound of me dropping the pen).

But wait - before you go. Did you notice something amiss?

Somewhere in the book are inaccuracies, a couple of snippets of erroneousness. Did you detect any? All you need to do to be in with a chance of winning a prize is send an email to mmcewan@madasafish.com with a brief note of any one clanger.

That's it. Good luck.

Oh! And one last thing.

It makes all the difference to us authors when we receive a nice review. Please don't wait to do it later. Go to Amazon and say a few words about how you enjoyed it.

Thanks a million.

ACKNOWLEDGEMENTS & AUTHORS NOTE

A big slobbery kiss on his baldy heid for Donald Cowan as a thanks for his suggestions. A wee nip of his favourite malt for David Johnstone and a bow to his superior knowledge and helpful advice. Copious pints of Guinness and a packet of crisps for Wilson Tasker for his keen eye looking over my punctuation and spelling. A decaf and a flapjack anytime she likes for Jackie Stewart in appreciation of her promotional skills, time and encouragement. A great big hug and a cup of tea every fifteen minutes for number two son who put together dozens of book cover designs and the brilliant one we settled on. A special thanks to my wife, who continues to put up with me sitting at my computer all day instead of forcing me to look for a real job.

I reserve my biggest thanks to you, the reader. It is your encouragement that has stopped me from getting a wee driving job to pass the time until I die.

I started taking notes for my police books a long time ago. I had no idea it would take so long to put them together into a book format. I reckon I took twenty-five years to write my first one. So I have every admiration for those writers who can publish one or two novels every year.

In the police, I worked with such great characters who gave me so many funny stories I felt it would be a shame if they were forgotten. I wrote the tales I wanted to hear, the stories I wanted to read and the lessons I wanted to learn. I am proud that I got them out of my head and into my books. Now I lie awake at night (insomnia is the scourge of a police career) and my mind still buzzes with ideas.

Also by Malky McEwan:-

THE REALLY FUNNY THING ABOUT BEING A COP

"I laughed so hard the tears ran down my leg." Irish reader.

"FIVE STAR RATING FOR THIS ONE. This is one of the best police books,it is very well written,very funny,and all believable.One book I did not want to come to the end of." - Amazon Customer.

"Just the sort of book to curl up with in winter nights, just don't have a cup of tea in your hand, as your likely to spill it, when you laugh, great to see the funny human side of the police, always be addressed problems within the police service, without sounding preachy, all politicians should read this book. Scottish banter at its very best!" - Kindle Customer.

"I read this book on holiday and laughed out loud on my wee lounger all day. A must read, even more so if you have worked in any of the Emergency Services. Witty and funny and a great read to make you smile." - Fiona

Here is an Excerpt:-

In the good old days, it was a regular occurrence for officers to be sent out on the beat and patrol the town centre on foot. It was a specific role for a crew to walk the town. Not just at weekends when discos were spilling out but every night, no matter the weather.

It wasn't a pleasant task to be night shift in winter and get the job of patrolling the town on foot. It could be bitter cold, or wet, or windy. It was particularly horrible when it was all three. Thus crafty officers used a few tricks to make it more bearable. They knew where to stand in the shelter, in a dry close or under a shop awning. A favourite spot was at the back of the bakers. The warmth of the ovens could take the chill from their bones, and the smell of the freshly baked bread was enough to have you salivating.

Another trick was to call in at the local clothing factory and cadge a cup of tea from the night shift security. It was a regular haunt of officers patrolling the town centre. We knew that we could get in out of the cold, receive a warm welcome and a hot cup of tea. The following could, therefore, have happened to any officer from our station; but it didn't happen to anyone, it happened to lucky old me.

One night PC Hill and I were sent out to walk the town. PC Hill was a gregarious fellow, just a few years older than me. The two of us worked well together, and he was always full of jokes and patter. Neither of us, however, really appreciated being sent out to walk the town centre on a quiet night mid week. It was cold, and a constant fine drizzle made it unpleasant to be outside. We had a quick jaunt through the town, confirmed that no-one was lingering about, then made our way to the local clothing factory security office. There we sat warming ourselves in front of the fire, drinking a welcome cup of piping hot tea, provided by the friendly security guards.

Unfortunately for us, the instruction to walk the town centre had come from the ambitious and overly strict Inspector McDuncan. He was a man that didn't take kindly to being crossed. Most cops worried about getting caught out by him but PC Hill just laughed it off, I fell in line. The security office was warm and dry. The security officers were chatty, and we remained hidden, happily drinking tea and swapping stories.

Then our radios crackled into life. "Where are you?" It was Inspector McDuncan.

PC Hill sat sprawling in his chair, feet up on a small table in front of him. He remained perfectly calm and radioed back telling Inspector McDuncan, "We are in the High Street checking the property."

"I'm in the High Street," Inspector McDuncan informed him, "… and I can't see you."

We sat bolt upright! "Er no Inspector we are checking round the back of the High Street, we will join you shortly."

Like sprinters out of the starting block, I followed PC Hill as we ran from the security office as fast as we could. We ran up the lane towards the town centre, crossed through the car park, raced around the Post Office and dodged through a close at the back of the High Street. The close took us out into the bottom of the High Street, yards from where Inspector McDuncan was waiting, arms folded and tapping his foot on the ground.

PC Hill and I stood in front of him desperately trying to hide our breathlessness. Inspector McDuncan looked angry, but we felt confident we had ran quickly enough to allay any of his suspicions.

Inspector McDuncan looked us up and down. "You have been hiding somewhere out the road, haven't you?" he challenged.

"No. No. Inspector, we were just checking the rear of the properties," PC Hill, answered for both us.

"You have been sitting somewhere drinking tea haven't you?" Inspector McDuncan challenged again.

"Not us inspector. We like to do our job thoroughly. More properties get broken into round the back, so we like to nose around there." PC Hill replied in as sincere a manner as he could muster. Surely his earnest explanation would be enough to hoodwink McDuncan.

Inspector McDuncan turned and looked me in the eye. "You have been sitting in the clothing factory security office drinking tea, haven't you?"

It was more of a statement than a question, but I felt obliged to stick to my senior colleague's story. I couldn't let PC Hill down, so I denied it.

"No, sir."

"Are you sure?"

"Yes, sir."

"Then why have you got a security officer's hat on?"

PC Hill looked at the hat I was wearing and groaned. We'd been rumbled. In a rush to get out of the security office, I had grabbed the wrong hat. I took the hat off my head, checked the band and saw there were no black and white checks where they should be. Instead, there was only a yellow band and the clothing factory logo. I wasn't in the least bit thankful for the bollocking I was about to receive.

The next day I came into work, got my gear from my locker and headed through to the briefing room. My entire shift was already there. No sooner had I entered the room they all sang;

"Where did you get that hat?
Where did you get that tile?
Isn't it a nobbly one, and just the proper style?
I should like to have one.
Just the same as that!
Where'er I go, they shout "Hello!
Where did you get that hat?"

Strangely, it was about then I felt accepted, just another one of the boys. Although, I would be hard pushed to be accepted as the hero of the day like PC Penfold - if only they knew what he had really been up to.

Available on Amazon

THE REALLY STUPID THING ABOUT BEING A SERGEANT

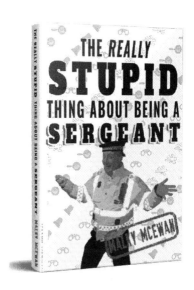

"A very enjoyable read this, many funny anecdotes but the best was the one about anger management, I was sniggering about that for the rest of the evening." - White Camel.

"I so enjoyed the first in this series I had to get the Sergeant sequel, and was not disappointed. Malky writes a really good yarn and helps me to start my day with a smile on my face. Another one please." - Carol

"He's done it again!! More stories of life on the beat, this time with some added responsibility as a Sergeant and some of the problems the cops create for you. A cracking read for the

A LITTLE PREAMBLE

People sometimes ask me if I ever got flashed or propositioned to get themselves off with a ticket. An innocuous question with a salacious undertone. A desire to hear some spicy scandal?

I got an eyeful, once, when I went to deal with a noisy music complaint.

The normal procedure is to alert the householder to the complaint and request they turn the volume down. Should they refuse or ignore the warning we can charge them with a nuisance offence and take possession of their music playing equipment - problem solved.

On this occasion, a young lady answered the door, in the background I could hear the music blaring. It wasn't the first time I had been to her home; she had regular parties that kept her neighbours awake to all hours of the morning. When she came to the door, she opened it wide and stood facing my colleague and me. She was wearing a see-through negligee that didn't even reach below the waist. There were three steps up to her front door and because I was standing on the bottom step, my eye-line was level with her bushy pudenda. As magnificent as it was, I averted my gaze and looked her in the eye. I asked her to step back into her house, out of sight, and requested that she dress herself before we spoke to her. She went inside but refused to dress herself.

Instead, she took a seat in her lounge chair, unperturbed by her near nakedness. I turned her stereo off, gave her a warning and my colleague and I made a quick exit. We were very professional. I stopped outside to note the details in my notebook and the circumstances. Maybe she wasn't trying to proposition us, she didn't make a show of her body, she just seemed comfortable being naked. I didn't grant her any favours; she received a warning like any other person.

On another occasion, night shift, alone in my office. A woman came to the door dressed in a fur coat. I didn't know her, other than I had seen her around the small town where I worked.

It turned out she was looking for the services of a police officer that wasn't part of our duties; there was nothing under that fur coat (other than a garter belt and high heels). She was a good looking woman, and I was flattered - that was until she spoke.

"Is Constable Herman not on tonight," she said, wrapping her fur coat tightly around herself when she realised she had mixed up his shift pattern.

I went scarlet.

However, the most shocking proposition I received wasn't to get out of a ticket, it was to get out of a bollocking.

I was duty sergeant and had to have a closed door session with a female cop. She was an experienced officer and good at her job. Not only was she an asset, she had a sparkling personality and made the workplace a happier place.

I had to reprimand her for something - it must have been a minor matter because I can't recall what it was. I remember her attitude to it though. She laughed it off, fluttered her eyelashes and told me she fancied me. There I was trying to be serious and professional. She couldn't care about the reprimand. Instead she suggested that I come back to her flat when we finished work.

I was aghast. How could she be so dismissive of my reprimand? What on earth possessed her to suggest such a thing to her sergeant? She must know I would not contemplate getting involved with a member of my team. That would have been totally unprofessional - a step into dangerous territory. It was a wholly improper suggestion. I need not tell you her proposal stunned me. I couldn't speak for a few seconds, appalled by her audacity.

She had a nice flat though!*

The *really* STUPID thing about being a SERGEANT is my second book detailing the funny incidents, the strange goings on, and the comic situations encountered during a thirty year and two-month career in the police. Guaranteed to make anyone with the slightest sense of humour laugh out loud. You can read these humorous accounts in any order. This book is worth reading for the one scene alone that had me, my custody assistant and every single prisoner in the custody suite laughing until our sides were sore; detailed in all its glory in the chapter entitled 'Hokey Cokey in the pokey'.

248

PC Penfold makes a return, but there are new characters too; Inspector Deadpan Dick who had me in stitches in a McDonald's drive-thru, Superintendent Amnesiac, and much more. There are even two bedroom scenes, the names have been changed, but my colleagues are utterly embarrassed when reminded of what went on.

*I couldn't resist this one liner - it is of course not true.**
** Her flat was actually a mess.

Available on Amazon

HOW TO BE THE MOST OUTSTANDING COP IN THE WORLD - IN A SILLY WAY

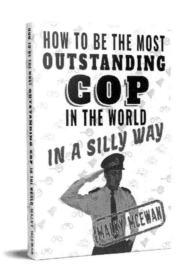

"This is the third in the trilogy and have to say, as an ex cop I enjoyed it thoroughly. It is entertaining, and shows the lighter side of what is an extremely serious profession (most of the time). Well worth the purchase if you fancy a light hearted read." - Kindle customer.

"I really hope that Malky tells lies and that this is NOT the final one. Another excellent series of tales and stories of his Police 'career.' A cracking read!" - Adrian

"Another great read, read his previous books and it just gets better. This proves the statement 'the polis really are human after all'. Put a bit of sun in your life, buy the book!!" - GerryH

A LITTLE PREAMBLE

I shouldn't be giving this one away because it is such a powerful technique - but nobody will read this, right?

If you ever get stopped while driving always tell the police officer, "I'm glad you stopped me because..."

That is a good start. It is non-confrontational. It will distract the officer from his original aim. Curious why you are glad he stopped you. That minor traffic offence you committed will go to the back of his mind.

The next part of the technique involves the 'why?'

Adapt the reason you give for being glad he stopped you to your situation. Your reason should fit in with what you are doing or where you are going. There should be no need to lie.

"I am looking for directions to..."
"Can you tell me where the nearest toilet/pharmacy/petrol station is?"
"I'm lost."
"I'm not feeling well."
"My car has been playing up."

Police officers join the job to help people. Redirecting their attention from issuing a minor ticket to helping a member of the public is something they would prefer to be doing. It makes them feel good to help others. It works at a base psychological level. Thus, if you get it right, they forget their reason for stopping you and assist you with your problem. As an afterthought, they might say something like; *'Oh, by the way, get your taillight fixed,'* or *'keep your speed down,'* or *'remember to use your indicator.'*

It is a win/win situation. The officer will feel good for helping you, and you get away with a quiet word in your ear. The method does not work if you fall out of your vehicle drunk or have committed a hit and run or other serious offence.

STOP PRESS:

This technique also does not work if, like me, you get stopped by a police officer who has read this book, therefore knows this modus operandi and doesn't believe you are bursting for the toilet (I wonder if I can sue for a new pair of trousers?).

So without further ado, here is my final effort in the trilogy of police memoirs documenting the amusing circumstances, crazy scrapes, nonsense and shenanigans that went on. There is no central plot to follow. You don't have to be a police officer to recognise the characters - they appear in every walk of life. You don't have to want to be an outstanding police officer either. I wrote this book to record the comical cases and hilarious situations I experienced during my thirty-year career in the police.

I changed the names to protect the guilty, embellished stories and took literary licence. Although, the most ludicrous stories are probably true.

THE MICHAEL PARKINSON TELEVISION INTERVIEW

British broadcaster Michael Parkinson (best known for his long-running talk show, *Parkinson*), said *'Muhammad Ali was the most extraordinary man I ever met'*. But who was the second?

The following happened when Michael Parkinson came out of retirement for one last chat show:-

Parky: I'd like to welcome to the studio tonight Malky McEwan, best-selling and award-winning author of *How to be the most outstanding cop in the world*.

APPLAUSE

Malky enters, embraces Parky and takes a seat.

Parky: Welcome, Malky. Can I call you Malky or should I call you Inspector McEwan?

Malky: Malky is fine. I'm no longer an inspector.

Parky: Now, Malky you have written *'How to be the most outstanding cop in the world'* do you think anyone can become an outstanding cop?

Malky: In a silly way, yes.

Parky: In a silly way?

Malky: Yes, in a silly way. That's the title of the book. *'How to be the most outstanding cop in the world - in a silly way!'*

Parky: I see. What I'm interested in sharing with the audience is your experience with the not so outstanding cops you came across in your career.

Malky: That's not fair. They were all outstanding… in their own way.

Parky: PC Penfold?

Malky: Er… um… Yes, PC Penfold, in his way was outstanding.

Parky: Not as a cop though.

Malky: Probably not.

Parky: In your previous books you have described cops who were a little inattentive. If there is a puddle on the road, they would step in it and get wet. There are others you described as unlucky; they see the puddle, sidestep to avoid it and still get soaked as a car drives through the puddle splashing them. You say PC Penfold was both inattentive and unlucky?

Malky: Yes. He would be the one that would jump the puddle to avoid getting wet, then land on a jobbie, slip and fall back into the puddle and then get splashed by the passing car.

Parky: Does he appear in this book?

Malky: He makes a brief appearance, yes. Like the time he they asked him to play in goal for the police football team.

Parky: What happened?

Malky: They were only ten minutes into the game and he had already let three goals passed him. He kicked the ball so far out of play it cleared the fence surrounding the ground. PC Penfold shouted, 'I'll get it,' chased after it, climbed the fence and didn't come back. Everyone thought he went to the pub. Nobody bothered because without him they only let in another two goals the whole game.

Parky: Oh that's funny?

Malky: That wasn't the funny part. The next week they were ten minutes into their next game when PC Penfold climbed back over the fence into the ground. He raised the ball above his head and shouted, 'Found it!'

Parky: So will the reader learn anything from him about being an outstanding cop?

Malky: Of course, learning from other people's mistakes is way better than learning from your own.

Parky: Is that how you learned to be an outstanding cop?

Malky: I don't profess to have been an outstanding cop. For me policing was like sex.

Parky: Like sex?

Malky: Yeah, I fumbled around for a bit, not really knowing what I was doing and I was never sure how long it would last - but, oh boy, it was fun!

Parky: Do you have any good advice for anyone who wants to join the police?

Malky: I think the main thing is to have good posture.

Parky: Good posture will make you a good police officer?

Malky: Pretty much, the two words that help there are 'nipples leading'.

Parky: Look the part, project a good image, I get the idea. So this book is all about the funny incidents that you came across?

Malky: The silly incidents, the crazy characters and the stupid things that happened, yes. I think reading about what happens in the police and thinking about how you will deal with those situations will prepare you for what you may encounter.

Parky: It pays to be prepared?

Malky: Yes, but if not - at least you will get a laugh.

Parky: So Malky, what was it like when you first got promoted to Inspector?

Available on Amazon

35489622R00148

Printed in Poland
by Amazon Fulfillment
Poland Sp. z o.o., Wrocław